CAMINO FINISTERRE

Camino Finisterre: Santiago de Compostela - Finisterre - Muxía
Anna Dintaman, David Landis
2nd edition, January 2025

Copyright © 2013-2025 Village to Village Press, LLC
Village to Village® is a registered trademark of Village to Village Press, LLC.

Village to Village Press, LLC, Harrisonburg, VA, USA
www.villagetovillagepress.com

Photographs/Diagrams
All photographs and diagrams © Village to Village Press, LLC

Cover Photographs by David Landis
Front: The end of the road at kilometer 0.00 before the Finisterre lighthouse
Back (left to right): Finisterre harbor, Santiago Cathedral, Approaching Finisterre
Inside title page: The path to Cabo Finisterre

ISBN: 978-1-947474-29-1
Library of Congress Control Number: 2018909415

Text, photographs, images and diagrams © Village to Village Press, LLC, 2013-2025
Map data based on openstreetmap.org, © OpenStreetMap contributors
Cover and book design by David Landis

All rights reserved. No part of this publication may be reproduced, stored in a retrieval system or transmitted in any form or any means, digital, electronic, mechanical, photocopying, recording or otherwise, except brief extracts for the purpose of review, without the written permission of the authors.

Disclaimer: *Every reasonable effort has been made to ensure that the information contained in this book is accurate. However, no guarantee is made regarding its accuracy or completeness. Reader assumes responsibility and liability for all actions in relation to using the provided information, including if actions result in injury, death, loss or damage of personal property or other complications.*

Note about town names: We generally use the Spanish name for cities and towns, though most also have a name or spelling in the local language (i.e. Finisterre/Fisterra). We occasionally use the local language name when it is the most prominent.

Visit **caminoguidebook.com** for more information.

Contents

Camino Route Network	4
The Camino Finisterre	6
Pilgrimage to Santiago	8
Travel on the Camino	12
Preparing to Walk the Camino	18
Santiago de Compostela	24

Camino Finisterre & Muxía, 115.5km
- 1: Santiago to Negreira, 21.9km..34
- 2: Negreira to Olveiroa, 33.5km..38
- 3: Olveiroa to Finisterre, 31.4km...42
- 3A: Olveiroa to Muxía, 32.8km...52
- 4: Finisterre to Muxía, 28.7km..56

Spanish Phrasebook	62
Notes	63
About the Authors	64
Legend	65

CAMINO DE SANTIAGO
ROUTE NETWORK

SPAIN & PORTUGAL
1) **Camino Francés** (800km, St-Jean-Pied-de-Port to Santiago)
2) **Camino Finisterre & Muxía** (90km, Santiago to Finisterre and Muxía)
3) **Camino Portugués** (610km, Lisboa to Santiago)
4) **Camino del Norte** (825km, Irún to Santiago)
5) **Camino Primitivo** (310km, Oviedo to Santiago)
6) **Camino Inglés** (110km, Ferrol to Santiago)
7) **Camino Invierno** (265km, Ponferrada to Santiago)
8a) **Vía de la Plata** & **8b) Camino Sanabrés** (1000km, Sevilla to Santiago)
9a) **Vía Augusta, 9b) Camino del Estrecho, 9c) Via Serrana**
   (circuit connecting Cádiz, Tarifa, Algeciras to Sevilla)
10) **Camino Mozárabe** (1500km, Almería/Málaga to Santiago)
11) **Camino de Levante** (1300km, Valencia to Santiago)
12) **Camino Aragonés** (170km, Samport Pass to Puente la Reina)
13) **Camino Catalán** (1250km, Barcelona area to Santiago)

FRANCE
14) **Chemin de Paris** (1000km, Paris to St-Jean)
15) **Chemin de Vézelay** (900km, Vézelay to St-Jean)
16) **Chemin de Le Puy** (730km, Le Puy to St-Jean)
17) **Chemin d'Arles** (740km, Arles to Samport pass)

Many other connecting routes exist from various locations in Europe.

*Pilgrims, poor or rich, whether coming or going to
the place of St. James, must be received charitably and
respected by all peoples. For whoever will take them
in and diligently procure hospitality for them, will be
hosting not only St. James but even the Lord Himself.*

Codex Calixtinus

ATLANTIC OCEAN

CAMINO FINISTERRE

Barefoot pilgrims enjoying the sandy beach to Finisterre on this pleasant and less populated path

Walk from Santiago de Compostela to Finisterre and Muxía along the wild *Costa da Morte* of Galicia. Lovely ocean views, mysterious shaded forests, and the lighthouse at "the end of the world" await.

◉ **EuroVelo 3:** Cyclists may choose to follow the signed EuroVelo 3 "Pilgrim's Route" which originates in Norway, and closely parallels the Camino Finisterre but uses more paved roads (the routes are MTB-friendly). **en.eurovelo.com/ev3**

An increasing number of pilgrims who reach Santiago keep walking to Finisterre, an additional 90km (3-4 days). Though fewer walk the additional day to Muxía (+28km), with its seaside church and Santiago lore. The path is well marked and considerably less populated than the Camino Francés. While services are fewer and farther between, the trek is not very difficult for a seasoned Camino hiker, with undulating hills, thick forests and quaint villages with stone fences. The landscape takes on the enchanting addition of the sea when approaching Finisterre and Muxía.

CAMINO FINISTERRE

The original roots of the Finisterre pilgrimage are not decisively known, though many speculate that it may have been a pre-Christian pilgrimage route to the *Ara Solis* at Cabo Finisterre (p. 272). Before Columbus stumbled upon the new world, the western coast of Spain was literally thought of as the "end of the world" (Latin: *finis* end, *terrae* earth).

Today the route to Finisterre is marked with yellow arrows as well as concrete milestones that indicate the distance to the coast. The waymarks from Santiago to Finisterre and from Hospital to Muxía are marked only in one direction (east to west), while the route from Finisterre to Muxía is marked in both directions. It is possible to walk Santiago-Muxía-Finisterre OR Santiago-Finisterre-Muxía. We recommend the latter, principally because of a delightful stretch of uninterrupted countryside between Hospital and Finisterre, though this book gives information for both itineraries. The trail can be walked any time of year, but May through September offer the longest daylight hours for covering the long distances. As in the rest of Galicia, rain is a constant possibility.

Pilgrim statue on the way to the Finisterre lighthouse

This additional trail can serve as an "epilogue" of sorts to a longer Camino, or holds its own as a standalone experience as well. The act of walking literally until the trail meets the sea can be helpful to shift gears and process the experience. In summer, hundreds of pilgrims gather at the lighthouse of Finisterre to watch the sun sink below the horizon and some followed a modern tradition of burning an item of clothing there to signify the end of the journey (no longer permitted). Both Finisterre and Muxía are pleasant seaside towns with affordable accommodation options if you choose to stay a few days. While the sea is often too wild here for swimming, the Galician food and culture make for interesting exploring.

CAMINO FINISTERRE

Pilgrims on the Way

The Camino de Santiago is often known in English as the Way of Saint James. The Spanish word *camino* can be translated as *trail*, *path*, *road* or even *journey*, but *way* serves a most accurate translation. This *way* is much broader and more expansive than any geographic track. Likewise, the Way of Saint James invites walkers not merely to a physical path, but to a way of life. The goal is not simply to arrive in Santiago de Compostela, but to be personally transformed and inspired. Charles Foster writes, "As conventional churchgoing plummets, the number of people taking to the road rises" (*The Sacred Journey*). Something draws this diverse group to leave behind the comfort of home for the unknown along the way.

To walk 500 miles across Spain sounds rather unbelievable—such a great task of endurance that only the most adventurous and inquisitive of freespirited youngsters might undertake. However, this way is growing exponentially and has almost reached the status of a rite of passage in Europe, not only for the young but for anyone with a longing for direction, renewal and challenge, a longing for pilgrimage.

The Camino is different than long-distance wilderness trails, such as the Appalachian Trail in the USA, which is often undertaken as a solitary wilderness expedition. While the Camino does pass through uninhabited wilderness, the path also traverses towns, villages and even urban centers. While it is possible to walk alone, more often the way is walked surrounded by others.

The great joy and gift of the Camino is in the people you meet along the way and the sense of connection to the millions that have gone before since medieval times. Come prepared to journey with a motley crew of pilgrims and seekers from many walks of life. Bring your burden and step into the river of people flowing to Santiago. Through the days and the miles, you will most certainly be transformed.

St. James and Spain

"[Jesus] saw two other brothers, James son of Zebedee and his brother John. They were in a boat with their father Zebedee, preparing their nets. Jesus called them, and immediately they left the boat and their father and followed him."

Matthew 4:21-22

In the New Testament, St. James is referred to as a disciple of Jesus who left his trade as a fisherman to follow Jesus. The Bible tells us little about him, save that he requested to be seated at the right hand of Jesus in heaven and was present at many important events such as the Transfiguration and Jesus weeping in the Garden of Gethsemane. The last biblical mention of James is of his martyrdom by Herod Agrippa in 44CE.

INTRODUCTION TO THE ROUTE

St. James became known as the patron saint of Spain not from biblical account, but from tradition, oral history, legend and myth. The story goes that James preached unsuccessfully in Iberia and attracted only seven disciples. The Virgin Mary appeared to James with the pillar to which Jesus was tied to be whipped and instructed him to build a church in Zaragoza, Spain. Shortly after his encounter with Mary, James returned to Jerusalem and was martyred, and his body was transported to Spain on a stone ship without oars or sails, "carried by angels and the wind." The ship landed at Iria Flavia (present-day Padrón), and James' disciple met the ship there and transferred his body to be buried on a nearby hill.

The body of St. James was forgotten until 813CE when a Christian hermit named Pelayo saw a light that led him to the grave. The bishop authenticated these relics, and King Alfonso II built a chapel to the saint. The current cathedral was begun in the year 1075 and completed in the 1120s. The event that catapulted this modest shrine to a major pilgrimage site was the mythical Battle of Clavijo in 852, when St. James was said to have appeared to assist the Christian army against Muslim invaders. This story mirrors Muslim legends about Muhammad appearing in battle to assist the Muslim forces, who were said to carry Muhammad's relics. This image of St. James was a convenient motif to draw Christian support to the frontier of Christian-Muslim battle and to bolster interest and financial investment in maintaining Christian domination of Iberia.

Santiago, Rome and Jerusalem

Pilgrimage to Santiago continued to increase, reaching its zenith in the 11th-12th centuries, with reports of 1,000 pilgrims a day visiting the cathedral of Santiago de Compostela. Interest in relics was very high during this time, and infrastructure for pilgrims increased, including the establishment of the Spanish Military Order of Santiago to protect pilgrims. Many churches and monasteries provided accommodation for pious pilgrims. Santiago de Compostela became one of the three main Christian pilgrimage sites, along with Rome and Jerusalem. Since Jerusalem at times was a dangerous destination and the pilgrimage to Rome was mainly taken by boat, Santiago became the preferred pilgrimage site as it could be walked to from almost any site in Europe (routes on p. 4-5).

Early Medieval Pilgrims

For most medieval pilgrims, the journey to Santiago entailed a grueling journey of six months to one year. As today, pilgrims came with diverse motivations, such as *orandi causa*—in order to pray, to seek forgiveness, to fulfill a vow, or to petition St. James for a certain blessing, such as healing. The pilgrimage was sometimes "prescribed" by a priest or religious official as penance for a crime committed.

CAMINO FINISTERRE

Given the provincial lives of many peasants who rarely left their own tiny villages, the pilgrimage must have been attractive as an adventure that could be justified with pious purposes.

Pilgrims came from all strata of society, from royalty and wealthy landowners by horse and carriage, to middle class artisans and workers on horseback, to peasants, paupers and beggars on foot. Medieval pilgrims carried coins sewn into the lining of their cloaks and were often easy prey for thieves and dishonest money changers.

Medieval pilgrims had a certain style of dress that can still be noted in pilgrim depictions. Pilgrims wore short cloaks so as not to interfere with walking but to still provide warmth. A wide-brimmed hat protected from both sun and rain. Leather shoes needed frequent repair, so towns were often lined with cobblers.

Pilgrims carried several symbolic items. The ***bordón***, a wooden staff with a metal point on the bottom and a hook for hanging a drinking gourd, was symbolic of the wood of Christ's cross. The ***escarcela***, a leather bag that was flat and narrower at the top than the bottom, reminded pilgrims to carry little and rely on God's provision. The final symbolic item was the **scallop shell**. The *Codex Calixtinus* describes the shell as the fingers of an open hand, symbolizing the good deeds expected of a pilgrim. While medieval pilgrims only bore the symbol of the shell upon their return journey, today many pilgrims wear a shell on their way to Santiago.

Medieval pilgrimage was fraught with many dangers, including finding drinkable water, crossing rivers, exorbitant tolls, lice and fleas, bandits, thieves and murderers. For this reason, pilgrims traveled in groups made up almost entirely of men. Though

a few women completed the pilgrimage with their husbands, the pilgrim road was not considered a wholesome place for women. Most hospices provided large straw mattresses that were shared by dozens of people. These hardships were viewed as an integral part of the pilgrim experience, identifying with the *Via Dolorosa* or 'way of suffering' undertaken by Jesus on his way to the cross.

Images of St. James

In Christian art, St. James is usually portrayed as one of three images. First, James the Apostle often carries a book or scroll, and gives a sign of blessing with his right hand. James the pilgrim is portrayed wearing a pilgrim's traveling cloak with a staff, traveling hat, drinking gourd and the symbol of the scallop shell (p. 10). James the Moor-slayer is shown brandishing a sword and rearing back on a white horse, with the anguished faces of Moors beneath the horse's feet.

INTRODUCTION TO THE ROUTE

Codex Calixtinus: The First Camino Guidebook

The Codex Calixtinus, a collection of writings about Saint James, was written in the 12th century. The text provides fascinating insight into the trials and joys of medieval pilgrimage. The name "Calixtinus" comes from a letter introducing the volume, supposedly penned by Pope Callixtus II but thought to be forged. The Codex is a collection of five books, including the "traveler's guide," which describes stages, towns, accommodation, the character of local people, descriptions of local shrines, warnings of bad water sources and scams to avoid, and finally the city of Santiago de Compostela. The book was likely never used as a travel guide considering that most medieval pilgrims would have been illiterate and few copies existed. The entire text of book five, the traveler's guide, is available for free online.

Sacred Travel: Making your Trip a Pilgrimage

Prepare for an Inward Journey. While outward preparations, such as packing and purchasing plane tickets, are likely foremost on your mind, you may also wish to block out some time to mentally prepare for your journey. This might include spending a few hours in silence in a natural setting. You might write in a journal, reflecting on what has drawn you to embark on a pilgrimage and what you hope to find, experience or achieve. Other ways to prepare yourself could include reading from the Bible or other inspirational books, spending time in prayer and meditation and speaking about your pilgrimage with a trusted mentor or friend.

Focus on a Theme. Pay attention to themes that emerge as you prepare for pilgrimage. Think back over the past year and identify moments which were the most life giving for you and the most challenging. Medieval pilgrims were often seeking healing, penance or an answer to prayer. If you have been going through a difficult or traumatic time, perhaps your pilgrimage will center on seeking forgiveness, direction or peace. If you feel at a good place in life, perhaps the focus of your pilgrimage can be thankfulness. It can be helpful to choose a symbol that represents your theme and carry it with you on your journey.

Be Open to New Experiences and People. As you prepare for your pilgrimage, keep your eyes open and senses alert for surprises. Things will never all turn out as planned, but the challenges and inconveniences can also be a vehicle for learning. It can be helpful to think of each person you meet as a potential teacher, and be mindful of what you might learn from him or her. Remember, too, that your kind words, encouragement or assistance may impact others far more than you may realize. At its best, pilgrimage entails a community of people willing to care for one another.

CAMINO FINISTERRE

Pilgrim Practicalities

This information will get you started, and more extensive details are online.

Credencial (Pilgrim passport)
The *credencial* is a document that identifies the bearer as a pilgrim, with space for stamps from accommodations and sites along the Camino. A pilgrim passport is required in order to use the Camino's system of hostels (*albergues,* p. 14) and serves as proof of completing the pilgrimage (1-2 stamps per day are recommended). You may either apply for a *credencial* ahead of time via a Camino organization in your home country, or pick one up at any of the larger cities along the Camino at the pilgrim office or main albergue. It's required to use an official *credencial* issued by the pilgrim office in Santiago or an affiliated organization, such as the American Pilgrims on the Camino, in order to receive the *Compostela*.

Backpacks lined up until albergue opening time

Compostela (certificate of completion)
The *Compostela* is a document of completion awarded to those who walk at least 100km ending in Santiago or bicycle at least 200km. Unfortunately, the walk from Santiago to Finisterre and/or Muxía does not qualify for a Compostela (unless you also walk back to Santiago). Bring your completed *credencial* to the pilgrim office in Santiago to receive the Compostela, written in Latin and personalized with your name and date. The pilgrim office now has a QR code for registration to monitor your place in line. The Compostela is by donation; you may also purchase a certificate of distance for €3. If you indicate that you had no spiritual or seeking purpose to your journey, you will receive an alternate unadorned certificate. Credenciales and tubes for secure transport are also available for a few euros.

When to Go and Time Necessary

When should I go? While the Camino can be walked in any season, weather and hiker volume are the main factors to consider. Refer to the average temperature and rainfall charts in each regional introduction for a better idea of typical weather. Spring and fall are generally considered the best times as temperatures are normally pleasant and most services are open, however, the trail has become more crowded during these seasons. Summer can be quite hot, but the long daylight hours allow plenty of walking time.

May through September can be very crowded, with some competition for albergue beds. Many private albergues can be reserved in advance, and a variety of hotels and other non-albergue accommodations provide options. Winter is the

TRAVEL ON THE CAMINO

least popular season due to the cold and potentially rainy, snowy or icy weather. Most albergues and many other services are closed in the winter, though hearty winter pilgrims also report deep satisfaction in completing their pilgrimage under challenging winter conditions.

How much time do I need? This full itinerary from St. Jean to Santiago requires a bare minimum of four weeks (not including Finisterre). At least five weeks allows for rest days and shorter days when necessary. An extra 3-4 days to continue to Finisterre are recommended. We have split up the journey to Santiago into 31 daily stages, with an average daily distance of 25km (15.6mi), allowing for a 5-week journey with four rest days. Feel free to deviate from this pace, staying at intermediary accommodations, which are noted on maps and in the text. See our website for itinerary suggestions for a "slow" Camino of 40 days averaging 20km/12.5 miles per day, and a "fast" option of 26 days averaging 30km/18.3 miles per day.

Visas and Entry

Spain is one of the 27 *Schengen* states of Europe that have no internal borders. A new travel authorization system, known as **ETIAS**, is slated to begin some time in 2025. Travelers who were previously eligible for entrance on arrival, then will need to submit an ETIAS application ahead of time and pay a fee of €7 (free for <18 and >70). The authorization carries a limit of 90 days in any 180 day period (same as the previous visa system). Visit the ETIAS website or check with your embassy or consulate for visa-related questions. ⚠ Check for relevant travel updates at **caminoguidebook.com**.

Collecting stamps in the credencial

CAMINO FINISTERRE

Sleeping A H A 🛏️ 🔗

One of the unique features of the Camino routes is the network of affordable pilgrim lodging known as ***albergues.*** Albergues are simple **dormitory accommodations** intended for non-motorized pilgrims (traveling on foot, by bicycle or on horse). They are generally operated by the local municipality, parish, pilgrim confraternity, or a private owner. Many operate on a first-come first-serve basis, though most private albergues accept reservations. Lower cost albergues often fill up quite early in the day during popular seasons. In Galicia, most public albergues are operated by the Xunta (governing body) and have a standardized price of €10. They tend to be basic, and kitchens often lack cookware.

Costs typically range between €10-18 per person, with a few on a donation basis (*donativo*). Amenities range from very basic to all the "bells and whistles" like wifi, washer, dryer, guest kitchen, etc. Amenities are shown in the text through symbols (legend in back cover). Accommodations with their own website have a 🔗 symbol (links listed at **caminoguidebook.com**). Unless otherwise noted, assume that all albergues offer a mattress, pillow, bathroom with shower, and a place to handwash clothing. It's expected that you will bring a sleeping bag or sleep sack. The person in charge of an albergue is called a *hospitalero* (male) or *hospitalera* (female), and is often a volunteer. In areas with fewer dedicated pilgrim services, **hotels** and **pensions** often offer special pilgrim prices.

Spain offers a wide range of accommodations, from simple rooms with shared bathrooms in family-run pensions to opulent hotels. **A Hostel/Albergue** prices refer to a dormitory bed. If a hostel also has **A H private rooms**, the prices indicate <u>dorm bed</u>/<u>single room</u>/<u>double room</u> prices (€12/35/55). For **H hotels**, we list the <u>single (if available)</u>/<u>double</u> prices per room. Most albergues are open from around April 1 to November 1, with some staying open year round. There are few formal **A campgrounds** on the route, but carrying a tent is uncommon as "wild camping" is not generally permitted, and reasonably-priced lodging is available each night.

Eating 🍽️🏪

Typical Spanish meal times are breakfast at 10am, a large lunch around 2pm (followed by a *siesta*) and light dinner at 10-11pm. This schedule is directly opposite to the pilgrim walking schedule. Most pilgrims have been on the road several hours by 10am and are fast asleep by 10pm. Restaurants along the Camino have adapted to the pilgrim schedule and offer meals accordingly. Spanish bars (synonymous with cafés) are generally open all day, offering drinks, sandwiches, and light foods. On maps in this book, we do not distinguish between bars/cafés and restaurants, as both normally offer drinks and food.

TRAVEL ON THE CAMINO

A **Spanish breakfast** usually consists of coffee with a little toast or a pastry, no full English breakfast or greasy diner to be found. Consider carrying extra food if you are accustomed to more filling breakfasts. A wedge of Spanish tortilla (a hearty egg and potato omelet) can often be found for a more substantial morning meal. A **packed lunch from a grocery store** is convenient, as you can stop and eat when you feel hungry. Bars and restaurants usually offer sandwiches (a lot of ham and cheese).

Snacks for the road: The ideal snacks for backpacking are calorie-dense, provide carbohydrates and protein and have light packaging. Eat fresh fruits and vegetables for nutrition and to help maintain hydration. Nuts and dried fruit make a filling snack with protein and a kick of sugar. A mix of salty and sweet snacks can help maintain electrolyte balance, especially on hot days.

Lunch & Snack Ideas

- Granola bars
- Chocolate
- Tuna or canned meat
- Nuts and seeds
- Dried fruit
- Olives
- Salami
- Peanut butter and jelly
- Drink mix (electrolytes)
- Fruits/vegetables

The typical **evening meal** on the Camino is the *menú peregrino* or pilgrim menu. These set menus typically feature a hearty appetizer, main course, dessert, wine, water and bread for €10-15. Meals tend to be ample and filling, but focus more on quantity than quality and tend to feature a hearty side of French fries/chips. *Platos combinados* (plates with various combinations of foods) provide another more economical meal choice for lunch or dinner.

Another option is to **cook your own evening meal**. Grocery prices are reasonable in Spain, and a simple pasta meal can cost very little. In albergue kitchens there is often a shelf of leftover pilgrim staples, such as pasta, rice, oil and spices. Usually albergues with kitchens have a variety of useful pots and pans, plates, dishes and utensils. However, in Galicia the kitchens are almost always devoid of cookware, and it may be worth bringing your own on these sections if cooking for yourself is a priority. Note that since Covid-19 many shared kitchens are not available.

Restaurants and **supermarkets** are readily available along the Camino. Some small towns do not have a shop, but almost every town with an albergue has at least one restaurant or cafe. Small village stores tend to be more expensive than in towns and cities but are locally owned and contribute to the local economy.

CAMINO FINISTERRE

Train:
Spain: Renfe
  www.renfe.com
France: SNCF
  www.sncf.com

Bus:
Alsa (major routes)
  www.alsa.com

Monbus
  (Finisterre/Muxía)
  www.monbus.es,
  ☏900929192

Transportation

The closest airports to the Finisterre route is Santiago de Compostela (SCQ) Airport, located in Lavacolla about 14km outside of the city center. City bus 6A has direct buses from Hórreo bus stop to the airport every ~40 min: 7:20am - 10pm (€1, 30 min, Tralusa Co ☏981581815). A private airport taxi costs €23. Monbus (☏900929192) operates daily buses to/from Muxía and Finisterre from Santiago. Santiago also has train connections to major cities like Barcelona and Madrid. Local buses (Monbus and Grupo Ferrín) connect Santiago with Finisterre and Muxía as well as several other towns along the route. Towns and cities with daily transport access are labeled with respective symbols in stage chapters.

Money, Costs and Budgeting

The unit of **currency** in Spain and France is the euro, made up of 100 euro cents. Often the best way to obtain euro cash is via **cash machine/ATM**, which are available in all cities and most towns. ATM fees in Spain are on the rise, with many machines charging a €1-8 transaction fee as well as a less favorable exchange rate than the official rate. It's worth checking rates on various ATMs before withdrawal. Banks that are currently reported to have low or no fee include Abanca, Kutxabank, Unicaja, and iberCaja. Some debit cards have the benefit of reimbursing ATM fees, such as Charles Schwab. If an ATM offers you the choice of currency conversion at their rate, decline this as it provides a less favorable exchange rate.

Currency:
EU €1 ≈ USD $1.08
EU €1 ≈ GBP £0.85
EU €1 ≈ CAD $1.47

The main **daily costs** for pilgrims are food/drink and lodging since transportation is mainly by one's own feet. First aid supplies, laundry machines, historical sites and museums entrance fees may also add expenses. The Camino can be walked relatively inexpensively compared to typical European trips, especially if utilizing dormitories. A bare-bones budget of around **€30 a day is possible** if you stay in the cheaper albergues, get most of your food from grocery stores, and forgo extra luxuries. A more comfortable daily budget of **€50+ gives you more freedom** to eat in restaurants and seek out more comfortable lodging. Staying in **private rooms and eating in restaurants will likely require €70-100/day**. Numerous luxury lodging and fine dining opportunities exist for those with an even higher budget.

TRAVEL ON THE CAMINO

Phones and Internet

Most pilgrims carry a **mobile smartphone** for emergencies, contacting home, making reservations, taking photos, etc. While this is generally prudent, it's a good idea to make an effort to minimize phone time in order to be present in your pilgrimage, aware of your surroundings, and open to people around you.

The main options for having mobile phone coverage are **enabling international roaming** on your personal mobile phone plan, adding a **virtual e-SIM**, or purchasing a **Spanish SIM card** upon arrival (requires an unlocked phone). **International roaming** on US and Canada based plans may be expensive, but can be a good solution if only used in case of emergency. T-Mobile US has free, low-speed international data and messaging included on some plans. European plans tend to have inexpensive roaming within Europe. **e-SIM plans** can be purchased for mobile data only and are generally less expensive than international roaming from your carrier (consider Airalo and set it up at home before traveling).

The main mobile carriers in Spain are Movistar, Vodafone, Yoigo and Orange. Plans vary, and a prepaid SIM with minimal **data and call package** costs from €10-20. You only pay to make calls and send text message and are not charged to receive. **Messaging apps**, especially WhatsApp, as well as Facetime and Facebook Messenger are inexpensive ways to stay in touch.

Country codes and dialing internationally
- To call Spain (+34) from the USA: 011-34- (seven-digit number)
- To call the USA and Canada (+1) from abroad: 00-1- (ten-digit number)
- Spanish numbers have 9 digits including the area code: landlines begin with 9, mobile numbers begin with 6, toll free numbers begin with 900/901

Wifi ("wee-fee" in Spanish) is widely available along the Camino; most albergues and cafés offer free access.

Luggage Transfer and Tours

Transfer services cost **€5-10 per day** to pick up luggage at one accommodations and deliver it to the next. Weight (<15kg) and distance (<30km) restrictions often apply. Usually service must be facilitated with reservation-based private albergues or hotels, not municipal or parochial albergues. Remember to still carry water, snacks and a medical kit in a daypack during your walk. Several luggage transfer companies cover different areas of the trail. Private albergues usually can arrange the transfer with the company covering their area. You can book transfers online or by phone via El Camino con Correos (Spanish post office, 683440022), Caminofácil (610798138), or Jacotrans (610983205).

More planning info online at **caminoguidebook.com**

CAMINO FINISTERRE

Packing for the Road: Gear, Resupply and Navigation
He who would travel happily must travel light. -Antoine de Saint-Exupéry

A light load makes for a happy pilgrim, and weight should be a primary concern in packing. A popular guideline is to pack no more than 10% of your body weight. Resist the temptation to pack many extras "just in case." Shops are readily available in Spain and most anything lacking can be purchased along the way.

Backpacks: A 30-40L pack is sufficient for warm weather (40-60L for winter). Measure your torso length and choose a pack of the proper size, preferably being fitted at a knowledgeable outdoor retail store. Aim for a pack that weighs less than 3lb (1.5kg) when empty.

Footwear: Light boots or sturdy trail runners with a stiff or semi-rigid sole offer enough protection for your feet and ankles against the occasionally hard-surfaced, rocky and uneven path (trail surfaces, p. 26). Get fitted for footwear in the afternoon or evening to make sure footwear still fits after feet have expanded during the day. Bring some kind of lightweight footwear to wear in the evenings, such as flip-flops or foam sandals. ⚠ Be sure to test the fit of your footwear and break it in before beginning the Camino with practice hikes wearing your loaded pack. Invest in wool or synthetic socks (not cotton), which wick moisture away from your skin, dry quickly, insulate when wet and manage odor better. If you're prone to blisters, experiment with liner socks (wool or polypropylene) to create an extra rubbing layer other than your skin.

Sleeping Bags: For staying in dormitories, a lightweight sleeping bag or liner is needed, especially in cooler seasons. For winter and the cool edges of fall and spring, it's a good idea to have a 3-season sleeping bag. Buy the lightest bag you can afford within your temperature range. Hotels and other private rooms usualy provide sheets, blankets and towels. Some albergues provide blankets and disposable sheets, but not all.

Clothing: Consider hiking clothes as layers, with inner layers for moisture management, middle for insulation and outer for weather protection. The general rule for outdoor clothing is to avoid cotton as it dryies slowly and does not retain insulating properties when wet. Synthetic materials (polyester, nylon, spandex) and merino wool are preferred, especially in cold and wet weather. In warm seasons, choose lightweight breathable clothes that provide sun protection.

PREPARING TO WALK THE CAMINO

Be prepared for the sun with a wide-brimmed hat and **sunglasses** and use **sunscreen** regularly. Bring a **lightweight rain jacket** with a waterproof breathable membrane, or use a poncho that can also cover your backpack. Bring a waterproof pack cover or line your pack with plastic garbage bags to keep your gear dry. Pack electronics and documents in zippered plastic bags to protect against moisture.

Hypothermia is possible in wet, cool weather, so be prepared with a dry set of clothes (socks included) for after a rainy day, and bring one insulating layer, such as a warm fleece or down sweater.

Water and refills: While water is readily available most days of the Camino, it is important to carry sufficient amounts. Always carry at least one liter, and refill often; carry more than two liters on hot days or in more remote areas. Reliable water refill sites are marked on stage maps. Tap water in Spain is treated and drinkable *(potable)*. Most historic springs are marked as undrinkable *(no potable)* because they have not been treated or tested. Bottled water is widely available, but less environmentally friendly than refillable bottles.

Dehydration and heat-related illness: Dehydration can lead to fatigue, headaches, heat exhaustion and heat stroke (a dangerous and life-threatening condition). Be sure to eat foods that help to replenish electrolytes and consider an electrolyte drink, such as Aquarius™, on hot days. If you become dehydrated and overheated and are unable to cool down, take a break in a cool, shady place, rehydrate with electrolytes and cool with a wet cloth or fanning until you feel better.

Fitness and Training: While the Camino is not a technically challenging hike, the length of the journey and total distance walked day after day takes a toll on the body. By taking the time to train before beginning the pilgrimage, you will greatly reduce possible injuries. Training walks will help you get used to your hiking gear, the weight on your feet and shoulders, and any other potential issues you might be able to prevent. It's wise to get used to full-day walks, taking 2-3 shorter walks per week and one full-day walk weekly with your loaded backpack. Check with your doctor if you have concerns about your health or fitness level.

Blister Prevention: This very common injury can cause an end to your trip.
- At home: choose properly fitting footwear. Try on many options before buying (foot should not move or slip when walking on various terrain types and grades). Use wool socks and liners. Test footwear by taking hikes with a loaded pack prior to beginning the Camino.
- On the trail: keep feet cool and dry, take off shoes and socks for breaks, wash feet and socks daily, use liner socks.

CAMINO FINISTERRE

HIKING GEAR ESSENTIALS

- ☐ **Backpack** (30-40L)
- ☐ **Sleeping bag or bag liner**, lightweight
- ☐ **Navigation**: guidebook, GPS app
- ☐ **Headlamp** or flashlight/torch
- ☐ **Sun protection**: hat, sunglasses, sunscreen and lip balm
- ☐ **Towel**, lightweight travel type
- ☐ **Water bottles** and/or **hydration system** (2L)
- ☐ **Waterproof pack cover/poncho**
- ☐ **Pocket knife** (optional, in checked luggage)
- ☐ **Toiletries** (list opposite)
- ☐ **Personal items** (list opposite)
- ☐ **First aid kit** (list opposite)

Take the time to visit a quality outdoor gear shop to get fitted for a backpack that is comfortable and footwear that fits properly.

FOOTWEAR & CLOTHING

- ☐ **Footwear** (lightweight boots or trail runners)
- ☐ **Sandals** or flip-flops
- ☐ **Hiking socks** (2-3 pairs wool)
- ☐ **Sock liners** (1-2 pairs wicking)
- ☐ **Pants** (1-2 pairs quick-drying, zip-offs, or shorts)
- ☐ **Short-sleeved shirts**, tank tops (1-2)
- ☐ **Long-sleeved shirts** (1-2)
- ☐ **Light fleece** or jacket
- ☐ **Waterproof jacket** or poncho
- ☐ **Underwear** (3 pairs)
- ☐ **Sports bras** (2)
- ☐ **Bandana** or Buff
- ☐ **Swimsuit** (optional)
- ☐ **Warm hat***
- ☐ **Insulating jacket***
- ☐ **Long underwear** top/bottom*

*recommended for cooler seasons (Oct-Apr)

OPTIONAL OUTDOOR GEAR SUGGESTIONS

- ☐ **Hiking poles**: Used correctly, poles can take up to 25% pressure off of your leg joints. Poles are great for stability, especially going up and down hills, and serve double-duty as a means to chase away dogs. Worthwhile for anyone with joint issues. Inexpensive poles can be purchased in Spain.
- ☐ **Sleeping mat**: A lightweight foam pad can come in handy for sitting on and for sleeping if albergues are full. You can often find left behind mats for free along the Camino.
- ☐ **Pillowcase**: Most albergues have pillows but do not change the pillowcases regularly, a spare T-shirt can also be stretched over the pillow as a makeshift case, or consider a pillow-specific stuff sack.
- ☐ **Stuff sacks** or (cloth bags with drawstrings) don't weigh much and keep you organized.
- ☐ **Zippered plastic bags or waterproof stuff sacks** keep valuables and electronics dry.
- ☐ **Reusable nylon grocery bag**: Comes in handy as a laundry bag, purse and grocery bag.
- ☐ **Clothespins** or safety pins for hanging laundry.
- ☐ **Travel cooking pot and utensils**: Many of the albergues in Galicia have kitchens, but no kitchen equipment whatsoever. If you are intent on cooking your own dinners, you may wish to bring a lightweight cooking pot, or purchase one when you arrive in Galicia.
- ☐ **Camping gear:** Lightweight tent (TarpTent) or bivy sack, camping stove, a pot and utensils, and extra water carrying capacity. (See Camping p. 14).

*For recommendations on specific brands and models, visit caminoguidebook.com.
*Decathlon is a chain of outdoor gear retailers throughout Spain with stores in Pamplona, Logroño, Burgos and Santiago de Compostela, as well as Madrid and Barcelona.

TOILETRIES
Don't pack too much. Bring small refillable travel bottles of shampoo and conditioner <100mL/4oz.
Refill from items left behind (ask at the albergues) or buy your own refill and share.

- **Shampoo/conditioner** (100mL/4oz bottles)
- **Toothbrush** and **toothpaste** (travel sized)
- **Soap**, biodegradable bar or liquid, such as Dr. Bronner's™
- **Laundry detergent** (powder works well and weighs less) or 100mL/4 oz. bottle or solid bar
- **Toilet paper** or tissues
- **Deodorant** (optional, you will stink with or without it!)
- **Hand sanitizer**
- **Contact solution** (if necessary), replace at pharmacies

FIRST AID/MEDICAL KIT
Supplies are available in pharmacies throughout Spain and most albergues have a basic medical kit.
It's always best to be prepared with at least a few day's worth of each supply. Keep it light!

- Any **prescription medicine** you need
- Variety of **Band-Aids®/plasters, sterile gauze pads**
- Antiseptic towelettes or **wound disinfectant**
- **Antibiotic ointment**
- **Medical tape** and **Elastic bandage** (such as ACE™)
- **Pain reliever/fever reducer** (such as acetaminophen/paracetamol or ibuprofen)
- **Antihistamine** (such as diphenhydramine (Benadryl®)
- **Anti-diarrheal** medicine: loperamide hydrochloride (Imodium®)
- **Blister treatment** (such as Moleskin or Compeed®)
- **Safety pins**
- **Anti-chafing cream** or **baby powder**
- Small **scissors** and **tweezers**

TRAVEL AND ELECTRONICS

- **Travel wallet**: with passport/ID, health insurance card & vaccination documents, pilgrim passport, money, credit cards, ATM card, etc. Stash an extra ATM card or wad of cash somewhere separate from your wallet.
- **Earplugs**: high quality noise-canceling earplugs are essential for a good night's sleep.
- **Mobile phone** and **multi-port USB wall charger** (see Phones and Internet p. 20)
- **Plug/currency converter** for any electrical appliances (European plugs run on 220V with two round prongs. Most electronics run on 110-220V, labeled on device, requiring only a plug converter and not a currency converter.)
- **Portable battery bank** (10k mAh): You can charge the battery from outlets in common space without leaving your phone, and later charge your phone multiple times from the battery.
- **Headphones/earbuds**: Noise cancelling can be useful in noisy albergues. Bone conduction such as Shokz allow for listening while also maintaining situational awareness. Be very attentive if walking with headphones!
- **AirTag-style trackers** are helpful for keeping tabs on baggage and key items during travel.
- **Journal**: remember daily details and reflect more fully on the experience.
- **Book or e-Reader** for pleasure reading (just bring one book and trade when you're done).
- **Pilgrim's shell**

CAMINO FINISTERRE

The path is well marked with yellow arrows and signs.

Blister Treatment
Take a break, remove socks to let feet cool and dry out. Check for hot spots and address by applying moleskin, Compeed®, or duct tape to create an additional rubbing surface to protect the hot spot. If a blister forms, use a sterilized needle to puncture its edge near the skin and drain using sterile materials. Air dry and re-dress blister with sterile bandages. If the blister or surrounding area becomes infected over the course of several days (increasing red appearance, tenderness, pus, red streaks), see a doctor.

For **dry or cracked feet** from wearing sandals, consider wearing socks all the time to keep moisture in for cracks to heal. **Impact-related injuries** are common with the large amount of paved surfaces on the Camino. If your feet and joints are taking a pounding, consider reducing your daily distance, walking on the softer shoulder near the paved path or adding walking poles and/or thicker socks.

The Trail: The paths that make up the Camino Finisterre and Muxía vary greatly in trail surface, grade, landscape, ecosystem and climate. The Camino has more paved surfaces than many hikers expect, contributing to more stress on feet and joints. ▣ Paved/ Ⓤ Unpaved designations in this book refer to most obvious walking surface. Often there are unpaved shoulders or faint footpaths along paved roads.

Navigation, Waymarking, Maps & GPS → The Camino is well marked and among the easiest long-distance trails for navigation. The way is marked by a variety of official and unofficial signs, pointing to the final destination, Santiago de Compostela. (After Santiago, the Camino Finisterre markings point to the coast to Finisterre and Muxía). The most common waymarks are painted yellow arrows *(flechas amarillas)* →. Many other trail markers are used in different regions and cities, most incorporating yellow arrows or scallop shells on posts, signs and emblems on sidewalks and walls. The most difficult sections to navigate are through large cities, where routes are often poorly marked and Camino markers compete with other signs and may be blocked by pedestrians or cars. We've included a number of detailed city maps in this guide (maps are representative and not exhaustive, without every street name). **Interactive maps and GPS routes are on our website and linked with the Ride with GPS platform—which can be used for offline navigation on your smartphone or device.**

PREPARING TO WALK THE CAMINO

Daily Stages: This book organizes the Camino Finisterre from Santiago to Finisterre and Muxía into 4 daily stages averaging 29km (18 miles) per day. It is possible to walk to either Finisterre or Muxía in 4-5 dayss averagint 17-21km (10-13 miles) per day (see inside cover map for daily breakdowns. The page spreads introducing each stage include its stage map, elevation profile, total distance, total ascent and descent in meters (▲/▼), paved/unpaved (P/U) percentages, time estimate (☺), difficulty level (see below) and a list of towns with albergues. In the towns with an albergue list in the sidebar, the <u>stage's destination is underlined</u> and *towns with albergues at the beginning of the next stage are italicized*. This shows at a glance options for a shorter or longer stage, for maximum flexibility and customization.

Stage routes begin and end at the main albergue in each respective town. Cumulative stage distances are noted on the stage maps and correspond to distances listed in stage chapter text and town amenity boxes. Distances for off-route accommodations or points of interest are indicated with a plus symbol (example: +1.3km). Town amenity pullout boxes list resources available in each town, its albergues and a selection of private accommodations in varying price ranges. **Towns** that have amenity boxes have a dotted underline.

Distances are measured in metric units (kilometers/meters), and elevation in meters (m). In **elevation profiles,** note that vertical intervals vary stage to stage, and **relative scales are indicated with color-coded arrows on the lower left side:** ↕↕ ↕, which may not correspond to the stage's difficulty rating color (green is relatively flat, red is hilly). ☺ Estimated **walking time** for each stage assumes a pace of 3-5 km/hour (1.8-3 mph) with terrain and elevation considered. Factor extra time for breaks and exploration.

Each day's stage route is assigned a **difficulty level** from 1-3. These ratings consider an "average" walker, who is reasonably fit but not necessarily athletic or an experienced hiker. A "Challenging" stage will likely have some characteristics listed below. Exercise more caution in colder months (Nov-Mar) when snow, cold rain and hypothermia are greater possibilities.

Length:
1m = 1yd or 3ft
100m ≈ 100yd
1km = 0.62 miles
10km = 6.2 miles
1.6km = 1 mile

- **Easy:** Slight elevation change, sturdy footing, water easily accessible
- **Moderate:** More elevation change, steeper grades, longer distance, some challenging terrain
- **Challenging:** Significant elevation change, longer distances, some sections of rocky/loose/narrow paths with less stable footing, water sources may be scarce, trail is more remote and exposed (fewer shelter and services nearby in case of bad weather or emergencies)

Visit **caminoguidebook.com** for expanded planning information.

SANTIAGO DE COMPOSTELA

View of Santiago Cathedral from Alameda Park

"Compostella, the most excellent city of the Apostle, complete with all delights, having in its care the valuable body of St. James, on account of which it is recognised as the luckiest and noblest city in all Spain."

Codex Calixtinus

Whether beginning or ending in Santiago de Compostela, take time to explore this fascinating city with its iconic cathedral, wealth of history, and throngs of pilgrims.

💡 While most Camino routes end in Santiago de Compostela, the Finisterre route traditionally begins there. This magical and vibrant city has much to offer, including foremost the cathedral said to house the tomb of Saint James. Daily pilgrim Mass is offered at noon. 💡 With all the affordable private accommodation available in Santiago, we suggest a modest pensión or splurging on one of the fine hotels.

Historical evidence suggests that Santiago was once a Roman city, followed by Visigothic rule. The kings of Galicia and León were crowned here at the cathedral and Santiago became the capital of the kingdom of Galicia. The town was fortified in the 11th century after suffering attacks from the Muslims of Al Andalus. Santiago's rich architectural heritage demonstrates its role as the most important city in Galicia through the ages. Santiago's Old City was designated a UNESCO World Heritage Site in 1985.

The Santiago de Compostela cathedral (opposite)

CAMINO FINISTERRE

Catedral de Santiago de Compostela

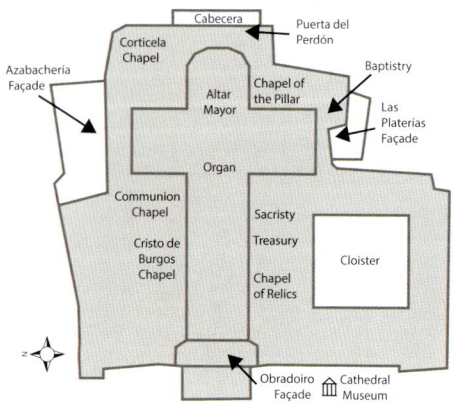

Catedral de Santiago

(free, ⏰7am-9pm, ☎981569327 ✉, ⏰7am-9pm, Pilgrim mass is held daily at 7:30am, 9:30am, noon and 7:30pm in Spanish, English mass at 10:30am at pilgrim office chapel). Pilgrims first head to the **Praza de Obradoiro**, the large open plaza facing the iconic western façade of the cathedral (featured on the euro coins €.05, €.02 and €.01). Medieval pilgrims gathered here and spent their first night in the city keeping vigil in the plaza or inside at the high altar. Fighting for the best spot was intense and in 1207 got so violent that the church had to be reconsecrated!

Next pilgrims entered via the west door, through the **Pórtico de la Gloria** by master sculptor Mateo. The Portico was restored in 2018 and is now housed in a separate area for climate control. You can visit by reserving a time in advance on the Cathedral website (free) or in combination with a museum entrance (€12/10 with credencial, purchase tickets in advance). Pilgrims touched their hand to the Tree of Jesse in the central column. While it is no longer permitted to touch, five finger holes have been worn away from millions of pilgrim hands. The sculpture of Master Mateo also bears the tradition that those who press their head against his will absorb some of his wisdom.

Pilgrims would then attend Mass and receive indulgences and make their offerings to Santiago and the chapels of other saints. The pilgrim would confess to a priest and obtain their **Compostela** (p. 12). Today you'll have to walk to the pilgrim office to receive yours.

Pilgrim Mass is held at the cathedral daily at noon. Get there at least 1 hour early if you want to get one of the 1,000 seats!

Worn finger grooves on the Tree of Jesse in the *Puerta de la Gloria*

SANTIAGO DE COMPOSTELA

The next ritual was to climb the small staircase behind the Altar Mayor to touch the **golden statue of Santiago**. Medieval pilgrims would place their hat on his head and their cloak over his shoulders. The statue used to have a golden crown that pilgrims would place on their own head, but the crown has been lost at some point. Today pilgrims usually give the statue a hug or lay their head against his shoulder, to whisper a prayer or message of thanks. Next, pilgrims descend to the **crypt**, with the bones of Saint James and his two followers. One tradition is to leave behind one's walking stick or other memento. Surprisingly, the bones of St. James were misplaced for almost 300 years before being returned to the crypt. In 1589 they were hidden elsewhere in the cathedral to protect from invaders. The bones were rediscovered and returned to the crypt in 1879.

The *botafumeiro* requires eight men to get going.

CAMINO FINISTERRE

During 🎗 **Holy Years** (when St. James Day of July 25 falls on a Sunday), the **Puerta del Perdón**, (the entrance on the east side), is opened and pilgrims can enter and leave through this door, receiving full indulgences (rather than the partial indulgences that an ordinary year bestows). The door is opened with great ceremony January 1 and closed with the same solemnity December 31.

Literally the "smoke-belcher," the **botafumeiro** is the largest censer for spreading incense smoke in the world. Weighing 80kg (175lb) and 1.6m (5ft) in height, the huge censer is swung back and forth from a pulley system above the altar, requiring eight men to reach speeds of 80kph. It is said the censer was installed to cover the stench of all the unwashed pilgrims. The censer is brought out for special days, though a donation of €500 is said to sponsor an extra showing.

Once your pilgrim obligations are complete, you can, like Domenici Laffi in the 17th century, "walk round the church, marveling greatly at everything." And there is much to marvel at here, one of the largest Romanesque churches in Europe, deceptively austere at first glance but with infinitely fascinating detail.

The Pre-Romanesque 9th-century structure that once stood here was burnt to the ground by Al-Mansur; the bells and gates were carried to Córdoba by Christian captives and incorporated into the Aljama Mosque. (The Christians had their revenge in 1236 when King Ferdinand won them back and had Muslim captives take them to the Toledo Cathedral).

The current structure was begun in 1075 and consecrated in 1128. The towers were added later in the mid-18th century and each depicts one of St. James' parents. The Baroque façade was also constructed at this time. Archaeological evidence suggests that a Roman temple to Jupiter may have stood on the same spot.

The southern façade is situated at the **Praza das Praterías** where, in times past, silver jewelry was

Since medieval times, Santiago de Compostela has been known for its *azabeche* (jet), a black stone made of petrified wood that is used to make jewelry.

Golden statue of Saint James in the Altar Mayor

SANTIAGO DE COMPOSTELA

sold. The portal here is particularly well preserved. The eastern façade features the **Puerta del Perdón**, and the northern façade features an 1122 Romanesque portal.

Inside, the golden **Altar Mayor** features images of Santiago in his three manifestations. Numerous chapels rich in imagery invite visitors to wander and explore. The cathedral is often packed out around the time of pilgrim Mass; consider visiting early in the morning for maximum peaceful atmosphere.

🏛 **Cathedral Museum**: (€10 for pilgrims, ☏902557812, ⏲Tues-Sat 10am-2pm 4-7pm, Sun 10am-2pm Mon closed) One ticket gets you into the museum permanent collection, Portico de la Gloria, Palacio de Gelmírez and temporary exhibits. Maestro Mateo designed the clever crypt underbelly in order to support the weight of the **Pórtico de Gloria** above. Sculptures are displayed amongst the architecture. The highlight of the treasury is a 1544 monstrance showing scenes from the life of Santiago. The museum contains a fantastic collection of medieval tapestries and other historical art. The museum also offers a worthwhile guided tour of decks and tower, as well as a night tour at 10:45pm (€25, reserve in advance).

Bagpipe player serenades visitors to Santiago de Compostela

Santiago has a wealth of other historical buildings and cultural experiences. Many visitors plan an extra day or two to enjoy the sites of this pilgrim city.

🅷🏛 Hostal de los Reyes Católicas

To the L when facing the cathedral from Praza do Obradoiro is the sumptuous Hostal de los Reyes Católicas, a 1501 pilgrim hospital commissioned by Ferdinand and Isabella, the *Reyes Católicas* ("Catholic monarchs"). The building served as hostel, infirmary, and orphanage. Under Franco, the splendid historic building with its Plateresque door was converted into a Parador, one of a series of luxury hotels throughout Spain using historic buildings.

Pilgrims gather in Praza do Obradoiro in front of the cathedral

☦ Monasterio de San Martín Pinario (✆981-574502)
Just north of the cathedral off Praza do Imaculada is the impressive Monasterio de San Martín Pinario. The Baroque façade is organized like a retablo and features an interesting staircase. The retablo mayor is very fine Baroque including images of Santiago. The ornate *Churrigueresque* altarpiece shows San Martín riding alongside St. James. Part of the monastery serves as accommodations, with good value pilgrim rooms.

🏛 Museo das Peregrinacións (Pilgrimage Museum)
(free, ⏱Tu-F 9:30am-8pm, Sa 11am-7:30pm, Su 10:15-2:45pm, *Rúa de San Miguel 4,* ✆981-581558) Interesting museum dedicated to the Santiago pilgrimage. The museum has a new exhibit at *Praza Praterías 2* including a cathedral model and an interactive video game where you can role-play a medieval pilgrim.

Be sure to try a slice or two of Tarta de Santiago, an almond cake dusted with confectioner's sugar in the shape of the Santiago cross.

🏛 Museo do Pobo Galego (Museum of the Galician People)
(free, ⏱Tu-Sa 10am-2pm and 4-7:30pm, Su 11am-3pm, *San Domingos de Bonaval,* ✆981-583620) This museum features artifacts from Galician history as far back as Celtic times, displayed in a 14th-century convent (Santo Domingo de Bonaval). The museum includes a Gothic chapel where several famous Galicians are entombed.

Platerías façade of Santiago cathedral

🏛 **Centro Galego de Arte Contemparánea** (Galician Center of Contemporary Art, free, ☉summer Tu-Su 12pm-9pm, winter Tu-Su 11am-8pm, *Rúa Ramón María del Valle Inclán*, ✆981-546619 ▣) Next to the Museo do Pobo Galego, this modern art museum shows a contemporary window into Galician life with high-quality exhibits.

Transportation from Santiago

✈ **Santiago de Compostela Airport** (SCQ) is located in Lavacolla, about 15km outside of Santiago. **City bus 6A** has direct buses from Hórreo bus stop to the airport every ~40 min: 7:20am-10pm (€1, 30 min, Tralusa Co ✆981581815, ▣). A **private taxi** to the airport costs €23. Numerous airlines offer inexpensive flights to major European cities.

🚆 **Santiago's train station** (*Rúa do Hórreo 75*, ✆902-240202) connects to most major city in Spain. The high speed *AVE* train to Madrid takes only 3 hours. Information at Renfe ▣

🚌 **Santiago's bus station** (*Rúa Clara Campoamor*, ✆981-542416) connects to most of the major hubs of Spain via **Alsa** and **Monbus** companies ▣, just south of the train station.

🎂 **July 25** is the patron saint day of Santiago, celebrated to the hilt with fireworks over the cathedral!

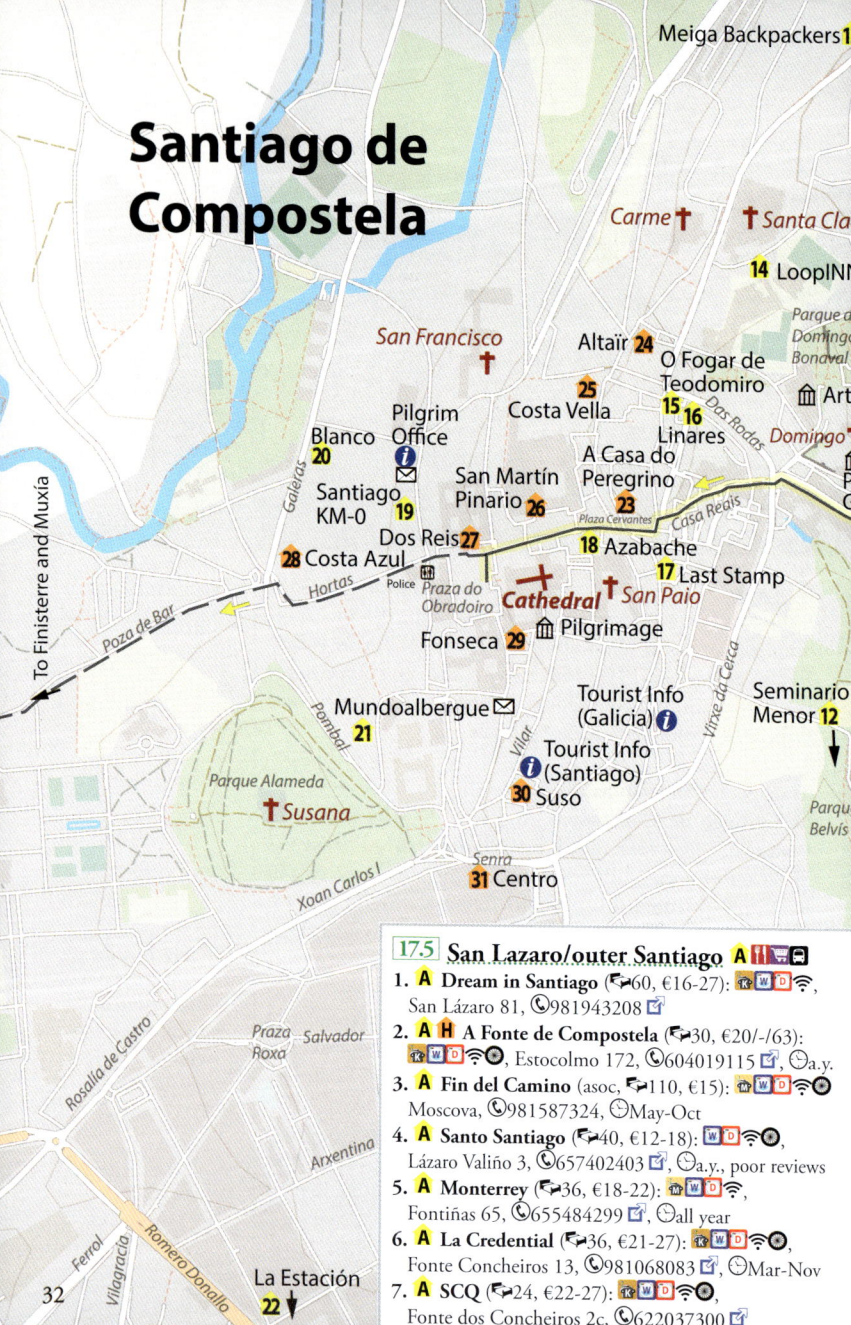

30.2 Santiago de Compostela 🅰 🅷 🛒 🍴 🍺 ⊕ € ⓘ 🚌 ✈

- Pilgrim office: Rúa Carretas 33, ☏981568846, ⊙9am-7pm (except Dec 25 & Jan 1),
- Santiago city: Rúa do Vilar 63, ☏981555129, ⊙Daily 10am-6pm
- Galicia: Plaza Mazarelos 15, ☏881866397, ⊙M-Sa 10am-5pm (closed Sundays)

1. 🅰 🅷 **Sixtos** (⌂40, €22-30/-/60): Fonte Concheiros 2, ☏881067936, ⊙Mar-Nov, no ⦿
2. 🅰 🅷 **Santos** (⌂24, €22-25/-/60): Concheiros 48, ☏881169386, ⊙Mar-Nov
3. 🅰 **Estrella de Santiago** (⌂24, €13-25): Concheiros 36-38, ☏881973926, ⊙a.y.
4. 🅰 **Porta Real** (⌂24, €22-25): Concheiros 10, ☏633610114, ⊙a.y., no bike storage
5. 🅰 🅷 **Seminario Menor** (⌂177, €22-24/26-28/52-56): Quiroga Palacios 2, ☏881031768, ⊙Mar-Oct, all beds not bunks, lockers available
6. 🅰 **Meiga Backpackers** (hostel, ⌂30, €19-26): Basquiños 67, ☏981570846, ⊙all year
7. 🅰 🅷 **LoopINN** (€19-26): Tras de Santa Clara, ☏981585667
8. 🅰 **Fogar de Teodomiro** (hstl, ⌂20, €19-25): Algalia Arriba 3, ☏981582920
9. 🅰 **Linares** (⌂14, €16-23): Algalia Abajo 34, ☏981580443
10. 🅰 **Last Stamp** (⌂54, €20-25): Preguntoiro 10, ☏981563525, ⊙mid Jan-mid Dec
11. 🅰 **Azabache** (⌂20, €24-30): Azabachería 15, ☏981071254, ⊙all year
12. 🅰 **Santiago KM-0** (⌂41, €27-32): das Carretas 11, ☏881974992
13. 🅰 🅷 **Blanco** (⌂20, €25/45/55): Galeras 30, ☏881976850
14. 🅰 **Mundoalbergue** (⌂34, €19-22): San Clemente 26, ☏981588625, ⊙all year
15. 🅰 **La Estación** (⌂24, €18-20): Xoana Nogueira 14, ☏981594624, ⊙all year
16. 🅷 **A Casa Do Peregrino** (€100-150): Azabacheria 2, ☏981573931
17. 🅷 **Altaïr Hotel** (€125-150): Loureiros 12, ☏981554712
18. 🅷 **Costa Vella** (€78-88/97-114): Porta da Pena 17, ☏981569530, restored Jesuit house
19. 🅷 ⭐ **San Martín Pinario** (pilgrim €29/45): Plaza Inmaculada 3, ☏981560282, call or email for pilgrim price
20. 🅷 **Dos Reis Católicos** (€280-350+): Praza do Obradoiro, ☏981582200, Parador
21. 🅷 **Costa Azul** (€38-41/64-71): Das Galeras 18, ☏602451906
22. 🅷 **Pensión Fonseca** (€34/60): Fonseca 1, ☏981584145
23. 🅷 **Hostal Suso** (€87-98): Villar 65, ☏981586611
24. 🅷 **Pensión Centro** (€40/55): Senra 11, ☏981588465

SANTIAGO COMPOSTELA TO NEGREIRA

1

21.9km (13.7mi)
▲ 478m / ▼ 561m

⏲ **5-6 Hours**
Difficulty: 🟧🟧⬜
🅿 72%, 15.7km
🆄 28%, 6.1km

🅰 **Albergues:**
Ventosa 9.9km
<u>Negreira 21.9km</u>
A Peña 29.6
Vilaserío 34.2km

Pilgrims enter Sarela on the Camino Finisterre

Walk through eucalyptus forests, picturesque traditional hamlets and over a legendary bridge.

💡 This shortest of Finisterre stages has been rerouted in recent years to reduce road walking to be about 1/3 on natural paths. Waymarking is generally good, similar to the Francés route. The climb after Aguapesada is steep and tiring! There are several cafés en route but few accommodations. The Xunta albergue fills early, but luckily other private albergues are nearby closer to the town center. Continue on to A Peña (7.7km) or Vilaserío (12.3km) for a more challenging day.

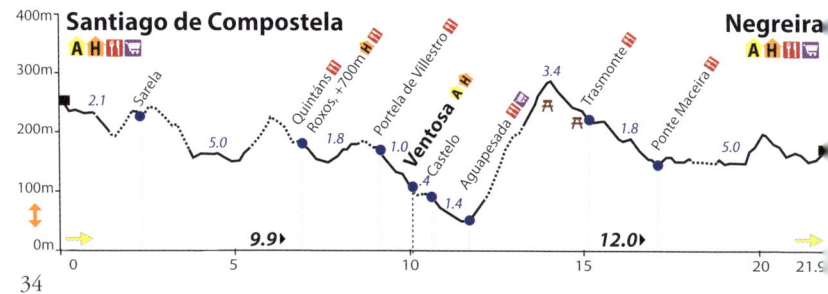

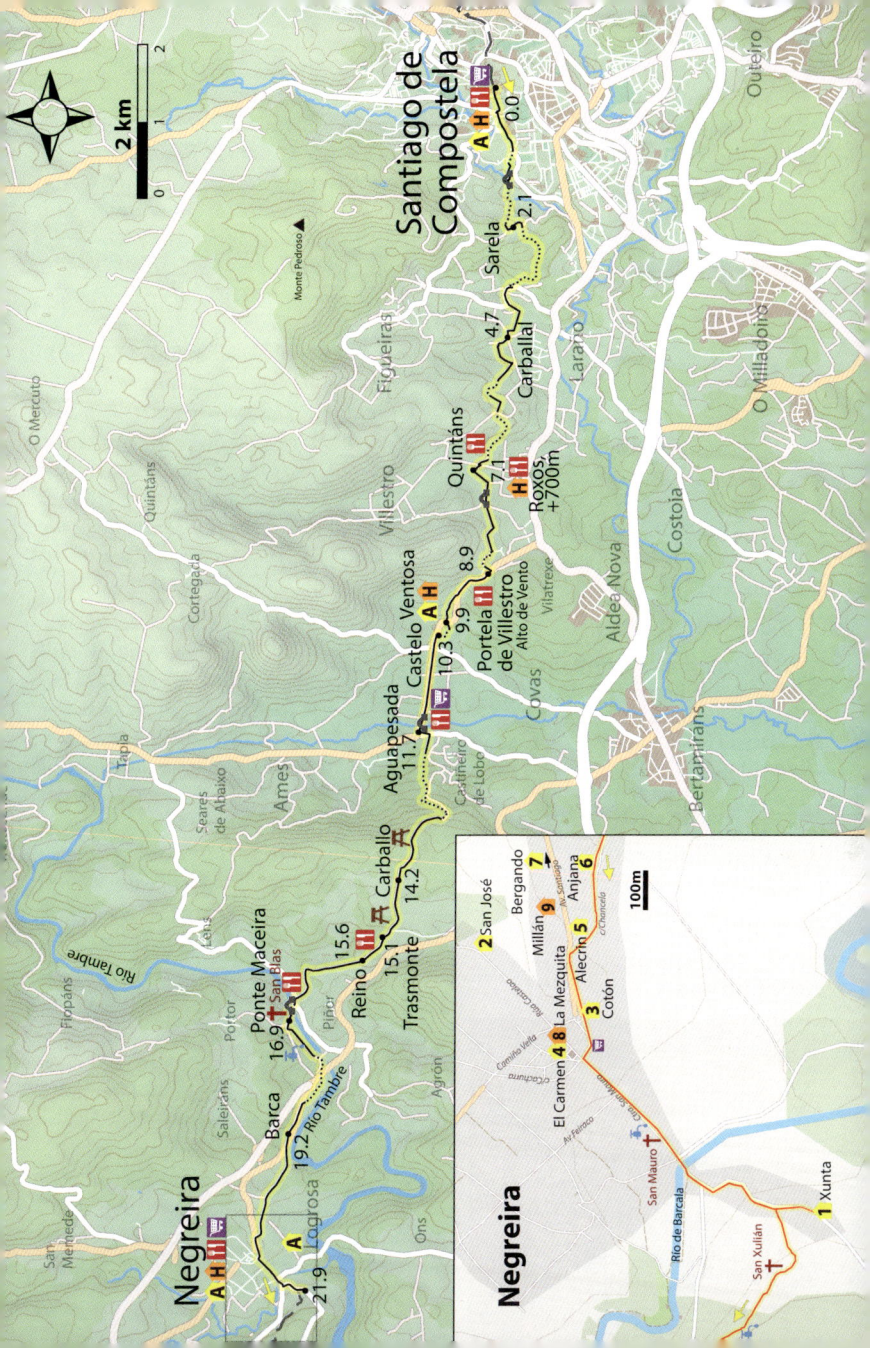

CAMINO FINISTERRE

0.0 *Leave Santiago (map p. 246) from the cathedral and walk downhill with the Parador to the R. Cross at Rúa do Pombol to Rúa de Poza de Bar. Turn R through green park Carballeira San Lorenzo with huge oak trees and the 1216* **Convento de San Lorenzo (1.0km).** *Cross a small stone bridge onto a dirt path. When the path comes to a T at a paved road, turn L into* **Sarela (2.1km).** *Be sure to take a look back at Santiago from this last vantage point. Turn R onto a gravel uphill path partway through town. Join a paved road that goes through* **Carballal (4.7km).** *After town join a small paved road, turning to dirt. Rejoin the paved road through* **Quintáns (7.1km)**, *where a* **detour to the south to Roxos** 🛏️🍴 **(+700m)** *is possible. Pass a rest area near a bridge, and return to dirt trail for a bit until passing* **Portela de Villestro** 🍴 **(8.9km).** *Follow the paved road over Alto de Vento through* **Ventosa (9.9km) and Castelo (10.3km).** *Continue along the road to pass by a neaby Roman Bridge into Aguapesada.*

Stone crucero

7.1 Roxos 🛏️🍴, +700m off route
🛏️ **El Asador de Roxos** (€65-118): 🍴📶,
Ctra de Muros 112, ☎981815973 📱

🛏️ **O Desvío** (€94/99): 🍴📶, Ctra de Muros 81,
☎981815994 📱

9.9 Ventosa 🅰️ 🛏️
🅰️🛏️ **A Casa do Boi** (🛏️16, €19-23/55-70):
🏧 🆆 🅳 📶 🅾️, Ventosa 92, ☎656490051 📱

11.7 Aguapesada 🛏️🍴 offers a pleasant halfway stop. *Now the trail begins to climb steeply on a dirt path through eucalyptus often accompanied by songbirds. Meet a paved road and continue on it through the town of* **Carballo (14.2km)**, *through agricultural fields past a picnic area up to* **Trasmonte** 🍴 **(15.1km).** *Continue on the paved road downhill through the hamlet of* **Reino (15.6km)** *to arrive to historic Ponte Maceira.*

Crossing Ponte Maceira
over the Río Tambre

16.9 Ponte Maceira 🍴 (📖 Galician: "Bridge of the Apple"), true to its name, features an attractive 13th-century bridge across the Río Tambre (restored in the 18th century). According to legend, St. James and his followers were fleeing from the Roman army. The saint's crew ran across a bridge at this spot, but the bridge was divinely destroyed after them, leaving the Roman soldiers stranded on the other side. The image of the broken bridge is

SANTIAGO DE COMPOSTELA TO NEGREIRA 1

featured on the coat of arms of the local council. Maceira was also the site of a 13th-century battle between the troops of Diego Xelmérez, archbishop of Compostela, and the fighters of Pedro Froilaz de Trava and his sons Fernando and Bermudo. The town is beautifully preserved, with streets lined with traditional mansions displaying family coats of arms. The cool waters offer an ideal spot to soak weary feet. At the far end of the bridge is the 18th-century Capilla de San Blas with a stone roadside cross.

Negreira wedding

*Turn L on a 1-lane road after town, which passes under an overpass and continues through agricultural fields to meet and cross the highway through **Barca (19.2km)**. Cross back over the highway and continue on the road into Negreira, with the turnoff (20.3km) for **Logrosa albergue** to the L.*

☀ Make sure you have enough supplies to make it to Cee in stage 3, the next full-service town.

20.3+ **Logrosa** A H ‖, **+700m off route**
A H De Logrosa (⛺8, €17/40/60): ‖ W D 🛜,
Logrosa 6, 📞981885820 📝, ⏱12pm all year

21.9 Negreira is a modern town with a full array of services, including some good seafood restaurants and the last full-size supermarket until Cee. The medieval *Pazo del Cotón* is an interesting historical marker with part of the original defensive wall, which adjoins the 18th-century Capilla de San Mauro. A modern sculpture depicts a man emigrating away from Galicia, a common story in the late 2000s when this region experienced high unemployment. On the far side of town, after the Xunta albergue, is the 18th-century Neoclassic Iglesia de San Xulián with a stone rollo.

21.9 **Negreira** A H ‖ 🛒 ✚ € 🏧 Pop. 7,077
1. A **Xunta** (⛺22, €10): 🅱, Patrocinio, 📞664081498, ⏱1pm all year, fills early
2. A H **San José** (⛺50, €15/26/37): 🅱 W D 🛜 Ⓞ, Castelao 20, 📞881976934 📝, ⏱all year, call in winter
3. A **Cotón** (⛺40, €15): 🅱 W D Ⓞ, Santiago 22, 📞881979654 📝
4. A **El Carmen** (⛺34, €15): ‖ W D 🛜, Carmen 2, 📞636129691 📝, ⏱12pm all year, same building as La Mezquita
5. A **Alecrin** (⛺40, €15): 🅱 W D 🛜, Santiago 52, 📞981818286 📝, ⏱Apr-Oct
6. A **Anjana** (⛺20, €15): 🅱 W D 🛜 Ⓞ, Chancela 39, 📞667204706 📝, ⏱Apr-Sept
7. A H **Bergando** (€20/-/64): 🅱 W D 🛜 Ⓞ, Mt. Bergando, 📞659447204 📝, +900m free shuttle
8. H **La Mezquita** (€42/60): ‖, Carmen 2, 📞636129691 📝
9. H **Hotel Millán** (€69/98): ‖ 🛜 🛏, Santiago, 📞981885201 📝

2

NEGREIRA TO OLVEIROA

33.5km (20.8mi)
▲ 638m / ▼ 531m

⊙ **8-10 Hours**
Difficulty:
P 63%, 21.2km
U 37%, 12.3km

A Albergues:
A Peña 7.7km
Vilaserío 12.3km
S. Mariña 20.4km
Lago 27.0km
P. Olveira 31.7km
Olveiroa 33.5km
Logoso 37.1km
Hospital 38.5km

Colorful garden after Negreira

Traverse tiny villages and beautiful gardens with decorated stone hórreos. Sleep in a traditional Galician building.

☼ This is the longest stage of the Finisterre route, and over two-thirds of the day is on paved roads. Stock up on needed food in Negreira as there are no shops, with only a few cafés and drinking sources en route. For a shorter day, consider staying in an intermediary albergue.

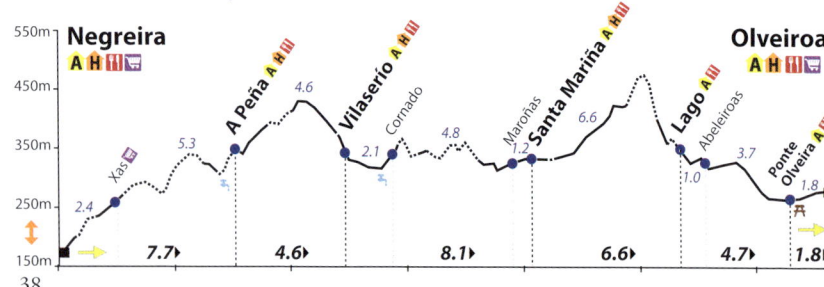

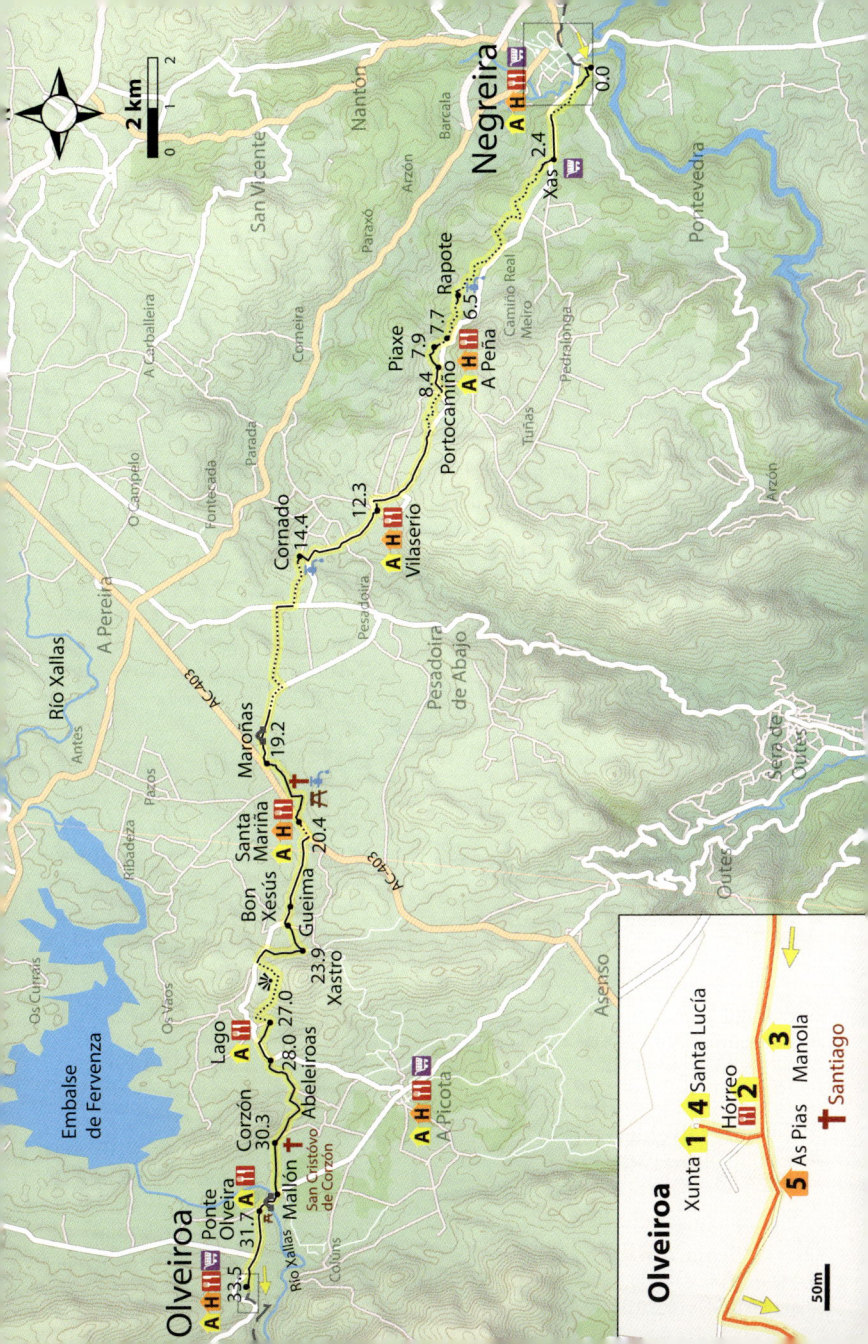

CAMINO FINISTERRE

7.7 A Peña A H 🍴
- A H **Alto da Peña** (🛏20, €17/-/50): 🍴 W D, Piaxe 5, ☎609853486, ⊙all year
- A H **San Mamede da Pena** (€17/40/60): 🛏 W D 📶 =, Piaxe 8, ☎649948014 📱, ⊙all year

12.3 Vilaserío A H 🍴 Pop. 72
- A H **O Rueiro** (🛏30, €15/-/60): 🍴 W D 📶, ☎981893561, ⊙Mar-Oct
- A H **Casa Vella** (🛏12, €14/35/50): 🍴🛏 W D ⊙, Vilaserío 23, ☎981893516 📱, vegan meals
- A **Municipal** (10 mats, don): very basic, at the end of town, dirty and uncared for

20.4 Santa Mariña A H 🍴
- A H **Casa Pepa** (🛏16, €15/45/50): 🍴 W D 📶, ☎981852881, ⊙all year
- A **Santa Mariña/Antelo** (🛏32, €15): 🍴🛏 W D 📶, ☎981852897, ⊙all year

27.0 Lago A 🍴
- A **Monte Aro** (🛏28, €17): 🍴 W D 📶, Lago 12, ☎682586157 📱, ⊙Mar-Nov

31.7 Ponte Olveira A 🍴 ▲
- A ▲ **Ponte Olveira** (🛏20, €17/-/45-60): 🛏 W D 📶 ⊙, P. Olveira 3, ☎981852135 📱, ⊙a.y.

23.9+ A Picota A H 🍴 🛒, +2.9km
- A **Picota** (🛏6, €15-20/-/45-70): 🛏 W D 📶, 13 de Abril 94, ☎981852019 📱, +2.9km, marked path

0.0 *From the Xunta albergue in Negreira, backtrack to turn up to the church and continue on a paved road to the forest, where it turns into a pleasant forest dirt path with pleasing views of the surrounding valleys. Meet a 2-lane road, turn R onto a narrow paved road at the mini market and continue through* **Xas** 🛒 *(2.4km), where evidently there was a dog wandering about on the wet cement! Leave Xas on a dirt road through field and forest. Skirt the town of Camiño Real and pass through* **Rapote** *(6.5km). Continue on dirt paths to* **A Peña** *(7.7km) and* **Piaxe** *(7.9km), joining a paved road. Soon windmills come into view ahead. Continue through* **Portocamiño** *(8.4km) before veering R onto a dirt path. Rejoin the 2-lane paved road until a dirt path to the L leads into Vilaserío.*

12.3 Vilaserío offers an early stopping point or rest stop. *Pass the private Vilaserío albergues and continue to* **Cornado** *(14.4km), where the trail turns to an earthen track to* **Maroñas** *(19.2km). Return to pavement and pass the Iglesia de Santa Mariña and a rest area before crossing AC-403 at Santa Mariña.*

20.4 Santa Mariña has a café, bakery, and two albergues along the highway. *Stay along the road and turn R to* **Bon Xesús** *(22.8km),* **Gueima** *(23.2km) and* **Xastro** *(23.9km). Return to dirt paths that climb a hill before descending to* **Lago** *(27.0). Follow pavement to* **Abeleiroas** *(28.0km)* *and turn R at the bus stop. The paved path arrives at a Y in **Corzón (30.3km)**, next to the church is ⛺ **Campamento Corzón** (air mattresses for €10/person): 🍴💧D 📶, ☎606817146 📇) with its Igrexa de San Cristóbal. Continue over a bridge to the main road. Turn R, with a special green lane for walkers. Pass through **Mallón (31.3km)** and over the Ponte Olveira bridge over the Río Xallas.*

Galician hórreo

31.7 Ponte Olveira has a café and albergue with a green lawn. *Continue on the main road until the signposted L turn into Olveiroa. The Xunta albergue is a short detour R.*

33.5 Olveiroa A H 🍴 Pop. 129
1. **A Xunta** (📞46, €10): 🏧, ☎658045242, 🕐1:30pm all year, restored traditional buildings
2. **A H Hórreo/Casa Loncho** (📞48, €15/-/50): 🍴🏧W D 🛒📶⊙, ☎981741673 📇, 🗓Mar-Nov
3. **A H Casa Manola** (📞16, €15/40/50): 🍴🏧W D 📶, ☎981741745 📇, 🗓all year
4. **A H Santa Lucía** (📞16, €12/25/35): 🏧W D 📶, ☎683190767 📇, 🗓all year, poor reports
5. **H As Pias** (€40/50-60): 🍴📶, ☎981741520 📇

33.5 Olveiroa is a charming traditional village said to have more *hórreos* than people. Observe magnificent examples of stone hórreos, some of which are beautifully illuminated at night. There is a small Igrexa Santiago as well as a stone *rollo*. Bar O Peregrino and Albergue Hórreo sell basic food supplies. The Xunta albergue is spread over several sensitively restored historic buildings. A nearby café offers pilgrim *menús*.

Detail of Galician hórreo

3

OLVEIROA TO FINISTERRE

31.4km (19.5mi)
▲ 471m / ▼ 728m

⏱ **7.5-9 Hours**
Difficulty: 🟧🟧⬜
P 41%, 12.9km
U 59%, 18.5km

A Albergues:
Logoso 3.6km
Hospital 5.0km
Cee 19.5km
San Roque 22.1km
Amarela 22.8km
Finisterre 31.4km

+3.2km (2mi)
▲ 110m / ▼ 18m

View of Finisterre

Relish a long stretch of earthen path in the wild Galician countryside. Catch your first glimpse of the sea and walk along the beach to arrive at the "end of the earth."

💡 Another long stage, but there are intermediate accommodations options. The day includes beautiful isolated walking through the high Galician countryside leading to stunning sea views. The route splits after Hospital, with the L path going to Finisterre and the R to Muxía (stage 3A). The path to Finisterre meanders along the beach to enter the city. From the Xunta albergue, the walk to the lighthouse is an additional 3.2km each way. Pilgrims gather at the lighthouse for sunset.

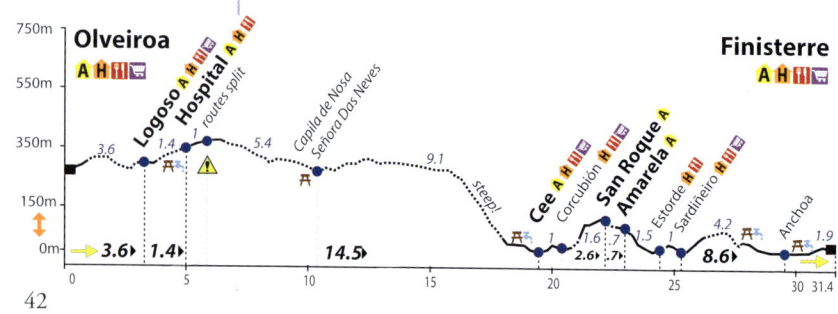

3 CAMINO FINISTERRE

3.6 Logoso A H 🍴
A H O Logoso (📞22, €15/50/55): 🅺🍴W D 🛜,
📞659505399, ⊙all year
H A Pedra (€50/55): 🏨🛜, Crta DP-3404,
📞652864623 ✉, +650m

5.0 Hospital A H 🍴
A H O Castelíño (📞18, €15/-/50):
🏨🍴W D 🛜◉, 📞615997169, ⊙all year,
 laster services until Cee, mixed reviews

0.0 *Leave Olveiroa on the main paved road, then turn L over a small bridge onto a dirt path. The trail climbs a beautiful windswept route with low-lying brush, pine trees and views of windmills. Cross a cement bridge to quiet Logoso.*

3.6 Logoso has a café, albergue and small shop in the same building. The town of Hospital is opposite the road on the R, where a pilgrim hospital was once located. A signboard describes the mythological **Vákner** beast, said to roam the forests of this area, with its first sighting by Bishop Martyr in 1489. Look for the Vákner statue by the cruceiro 3km after Hospital.

5.0 Hospital has the last services until Cee, and they know it! *Take the smaller paved road to the R after the café, which crosses the main road and brings you to a large roundabout where the path splits (6.0km).* ⚠ *Continue L for Finisterre past a monstrous carbide factory. In 500m, turn R onto a dirt path for 12km of heavenly walking in nature.*

10.4 Chapel: The path passes a stone *rollo* with a *Pietá* image (engraved CR for *Camino Real*) and the 18th-century Capela da Nosa Señora das Neves ("Our Lady of the Snow Chapel") with a peaceful sheltered picnic area. The water flowing here is said to be particularly beneficial to nursing mothers. A local pilgrimage to this spot takes place in September. *Continue uphill for a first glimpse of the ocean! Pass the nondescript* **Sanctuario de San Pedro Mártir (13.8km)**, *which also has a tradition of healing waters, said to cure arthritis in limbs that are submerged.*

Marker for the split: Finisterre or Muxía

A 100m detour is marked to the **Cruceiro do Armada (16.1km)**, *a recreation of an ancient stone cross. Views down to the bay are fantastic.* ⚠◉ *Caution on the very steep, loose track down to Cee. Toward the bay the path emerges along the waterfront. Several albergues make Cee an attractive overnight option.*

19.5 **Cee** A H 🍴 ☕ ⊕ € 🅱 Pop. 7,898
- **A O Bordón** (🛏24, €20): 🏠🅦🅓 📶, Camiños Chans, ☎981746574 📧, ⓧ12pm all year
- **A H Moreira** (🛏14, €15/-/40): 🏠🅦🅓 📶, Rosalía 75, ☎981746282 📧, ⓧMar-Oct
- **A Casa da Fonte** (🛏42, €15): 🏠🅦🅓 📶, Arriba 36, ☎981746663 📧, ⓧMar-Dec 15
- **A H A Tequerón** (🛏10, €16-18/45/50): 🅦🅓 📶, Arriba 31, ☎666119594
- **H Hotel Larry** (€50/70): 🍴📶, Magdalena 8, ☎981746441 📧
- **H La Marina** (€68-75): 🍴📶, Fernando Blanco 26, ☎981747381 📧
- **H Oca Ínsua** (€76-150): 🍴📶, Finisterre 82, ☎981747575 📧

20.5 **Corcubión** H 🍴🛒 ⊕ € ℹ 🅱
Pop. 1,767, 🏛 Celtic: "circular bay," ℹ Explanada do Porto 17, ☎981706163
- **H Pensión Beiramar** (€50-60/60-70): 📶, Finisterre 220, ☎981745040 📧
- **H Casa de Balea** (€89-105): 📶, Rafael Juan 44, ☎981746645 📧
- **H MarViva** (€80-100): 🍴📶, José Carrera 4, ☎628276773 📧
- **H As Hortensias** (€67-125): 🍴📶, Lg Praia de Quenxe, ☎981747584 📧, +800m
- **H Playa de Quenxe** (€55-120): 🍴📶, Lg Praia de Quenxe 43, ☎981706457 📧, +1km

45

3 CAMINO FINISTERRE

22.1 San Roque A - 22.8 Amarela A
- **A San Roque** (asoc, 16, don): 🍴, ☎679460942, communal meals, 4pm all year
- **A San Pedro** (4, €18/-/50): 📶, Amarela 17, ☎670395045, all year

24.3 Estorde
- **H Playa de Estorde** (€65/85): 🍴📶 ☎981745585
- **▲ Ruta Finisterre Camping** (tent €15): Playa de Estorde 216, ☎981-746302

25.3 Sardiñeiro
- **H Hotel Playa de Sardiñeiro** (€65-85): Coruña 68, ☎981743741
- **H Hotel Merendero** (€41/45): Alvariña 1, ☎981743535
- **H Playa Langosteira** (€65-220): Escaselas 1, ☎981706830

🎉 **Cee**
Spring: Galician literature festival
Summer: Street theatre festival
Sunday is market day.

🎉 **Corcubión**
April 25: San Marcos, patron saint celebration

Barefoot pilgrims enjoying the sandy beach

historically used for whale hunting. Much of the town was destroyed by Napoleon's troops, but the Igrexa da Santa Maria da Xunqueira was rebuilt in late Gothic style with traces of its original vault. *Continue along the water and up Rúa Alameda to Corcubión.*

20.5 Corcubión, sister town to Cee, is just up the road with additional accommodations and beaches. The Gothic Igrexa de San Marcos was built in the 14th century with later additions after being burned by Napoleon's troops. It contains a 15th-century image of the patron saint. Beautiful manor houses display historic coats of arms.

*At the church, turn R up the steps and continue to the Campo de Rollo plaza. Cross the plaza past a children's play area and look for a large yellow arrow pointing up a dirt lane with high walls on either side. Follow this path out of Corcubión, which joins a paved road and leads through the hamlet of **Vilar (21.5km)** to **San Roque (22.1km)**. Return to the road and continue onto an earthen path. Pass through **Amarela (22.8km)** and continue on a 2-lane paved road through Estorde and Sardiñeiro.*

24.3 Estorde and **25.3 Sardiñeiro** are both along the beach with restaurant and hotel options. *Leave town on a dirt footpath with elevated views of the sea, which rejoins the main road and then departs again to pass along the shore. The rest of the way into Finisterre can be walked on the sidewalk or by taking your shoes off and walking along the sandy beach. The beach **Praia da Langosteira** stretches about 2km prior to the entrance to Finisterre, passing the town of **Anchoa (29.5km)**. The Finisterre Xunta albergue is located in the center near the harbor and next to the bus station.*

OLVEIROA TO FINISTERRE 3

Finisterre has drawn mystics
seekers to its rocky shores for thousands of years. The Romans named it
is terrae, "the end of the earth" and,
ring out into the expanse of wild ocean
m the lighthouse on Monte Facho, it's
y to see how it may have felt that way.
tic pagans built an altar to the sun
a Solis) at Finisterre, and later Christians developed their own rituals around
s place. From the town to the lighthouse is 3.2km, and numerous footpaths
scross the peninsula's hilltop leading
interesting natural and religious sites.

is fishing village has grown as a tourist
stination with many accommodations
well as seafood restaurants, mostly
ated near the vibrant historic port.

31.4 Finisterre A H 🍴🛒➕€ℹ️🏛️

Pop. 4,983, 📖 Latin: *Finis Terrae* "the end of the world," (also Fisterra, Finisterra)
ℹ️ Tourism Office issues the *Fisterrana* certificate of completion (Rúa Real 2, ☎981740781).

1. **A** Xunta (⌂36, €10): 🛏️ W D, Real 2, ☎981740781, ⏰1pm, **kitchen closed 7pm-8am**
2. **A H** Oceanus (€17/-/40): 🛏️ W D 📶, A Coruña 33, ☎609821302
3. **A H** Cabo da Vila (⌂28, €17/55/66-86): 🛏️ W D 📶, A Coruña 13, ☎981740454, ⏰all year
4. **A** Sonia Buen Camino (⌂50, €17): 🍴 W D 📶, Atalaya 11, ☎981740771 ⏰all year
5. **A** Mar de Rostro (⌂23, €18): 🛏️ W D 📶, Alcalde Fernández 45, ☎637107765, ⏰Mar-Nov
6. **A H** Mar de Fora (⌂11, €18/-/60): 🛏️ W D 📶, Potiña 60, ☎686939079, ⏰all year
7. **A** Por Fin (⌂11, €19): 🛏️ W D 📶, Federico Ávila 19, ☎636764726, ⏰Apr-Nov
8. **A H** O Encontro (⌂18, €15/-/58): 🛏️ W, El Campo 7, ☎696503363, ⏰Apr-Nov
9. **A H** La Espiral (⌂12, €17/-/50): 🛏️ W 📶, Fonte Vella 19, ☎607684248, ⏰all year
10. **A** Ara Solis (⌂16, €15): 🛏️ W D 📶, Ara Solis 3, ☎638326869, ⏰all year
11. **A H** Finistellae (⌂20, €13/30/36): 🛏️ W D 📶, M. Lago País 7, ☎637821296, ⏰Apr-Oct
12. **A H** Fin da Terra e do Camiño (€15/25/40): 🛏️ W D 📶, Alfredo Saralegui 15, ☎67536189
13. **H** Hospedaje Lopez (€25-35/35-45): 📶, Carrasqueira 4, ☎981740449, sea views
14. **H** Hostal Mariquito (€55/70-80): 🍴, Santa Catalina 44, ☎981740044
15. **H** Pensión Fin da Terra (€45-55): 📶, Montarón 15, ☎648918929
16. **H** Hostal Rivas (€45/58): 📶, Alcalde Fernández 53, ☎981740027
17. **H** Hotel Ancora (€44/50): 🍴, Alcalde Fernández 65, ☎981740791
18. **H** O Semáforo (€120/144-350): 🍴📶, ☎981110210, in cape lighthouse (3km after town)

CAMINO FINISTERRE

The charming historic center has twisting streets perfect for exploring. Visit the **Castelo de San Carlos**, which has been transformed into a museum of local fishing culture. The 18th-century **Capela do Nosa Señora do Bo Suceso**, featuring a Baroque retable, is located in *Ara Solis Plaza*. On the way to the cape you'll pass the **Igrexa de Santa María das Areas**, originally built in the 12th century with funds from Doña Urraca, containing an image known as "Christ of the Golden Beard." According to legend, the image was sculpted by Nicodemus and was on a ship coming from England when a huge storm began. The sailors threw the statue into the ocean to ballast weight and the storm instantly stopped, apparently because the image wanted to make its home in Finisterre.

Cabo Finisterre

Take an extra day to explore Monte Facho further, which has marvelous views, wild beaches, and interesting historical sites. On the west side of Monte Facho, a series of massive rocks stand on stone outcroppings, known as the **Piedras Santas** ("Holy Rocks"). Two of these are known as the *Abalar* stones, which can both easily be moved back and forth if pushed on

Finisterre
July 25: Festa da Praia (beach festival)
Aug 20: Fin do Camino
Sept 8: Virxe do Carme

Picturesque fishing port of Finisterre

CAMINO FINISTERRE

Balancing on *Piedras Santas* on Cabo Finisterre

Fertility rock at Ermita San Guillerme

Sunset from Finisterre lighthouse (right)

in the right manner. This was the site of a pagan ritual where the moving rocks judged if a woman was apt to be a priestess. A Christian legend says Mary appeared to Santiago at this place to encourage him on his missionary journey. According to legend, the Celtic witch Orcavella lived in a stone tomb in this area and would lure hapless shepherds in and use them as a mattress.

In the 11th century, **San Guillermo** (St. William of Penacorada) built a hermitage on Monte Facho. Its ruins remain, and a particular rock is believed by tradition to enhance fertility, and it is said that couples hoping to conceive come at night to copulate on it.

0.0 Lighthouse at the End of the World

On arrival in Finisterre, you may wish to check into an accommodation before embarking on the 6.4km round-trip journey to the lighthouse, where many gather to watch the sun sink below the endless watery horizon. One modern pilgrim ritual was to burn shoes or clothing to symbolize the end of the pilgrimage, though this is now strictly prohibited.

The setting sun at Finisterre serves as an appropriate symbol of the ending of the journey and an atmospheric setting to ponder the return trip and transition to whatever is next. Rest assured that millions before you, and likely millions after, have pondered the same questions and perhaps felt the same bittersweet emotions upon reflecting on the pilgrimage. Revel in the satisfaction of completing such an expedition. Give thanks for the people you have met along the way. Grieve the ending of this journey, and welcome the dawn of the next.

The Finisterre-Santiago bus is operated by Monbus with multiple daily departures (€7.20, can be booked in advance: 900929192). Note travel time, as some buses are direct (2 hours) while others service coastal villages over 3+ hours. You can also walk one day further to Muxía (stage 4).

To process your Camino experience for a few days, author Tracy Saunders offers her house near Muxía, called *A Casa Do Raposito* (The Little Fox House), as a post-Camino retreat on a donation basis. Arrange in advance: ☏686315328 📱

The end of the road at kilometer 0.00 before the Finisterre lighthouse

3A

OLVEIROA TO MUXÍA

32.8km (19.4mi)
▲ 551m / ▼ 811m

⏱ **7-9 Hours**
Difficulty: ▭▬▭
🅿 50%, 16.5km
Ⓤ 50%, 16.3km

A Albergues:
Logoso 3.6km
Hospital 5.0km
Dumbría 9.7km
A Grixa 17.2km
Ozón 21.7km
Muxía 32.8km

Rooftop crosses at
Iglesia San Martiño

Walk through rolling countryside, delight in magnificent sea views, and visit the holy rocks on Muxía peninsula.

☀ This route is only marked thoroughly in one direction, from Olveiroa to Muxía, so if returning from Muxía this way be extra aware of reversed arrows and surroundings and consider GPS navigation. This route is less popular than the way to Finisterre (stage 3) and feels more remote and wild. Dumbría has an impressive albergue that usually has space. Walk out to the Muxía church at sunset for a fulfilling end to the day.

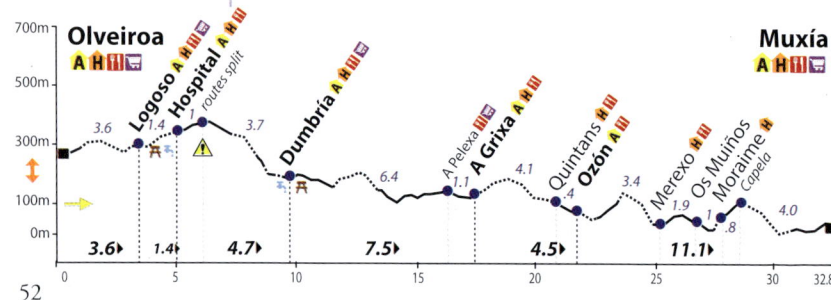

3A CAMINO FINISTERRE

Ubiquitous eucalyptus forest before Muxía

0.0 *For the description from Olveiroa to the **trail junction (6.0km)**, see p. 42.* ⚠ *From the split after **Hospital**, take the R option along the road then turn off to the L onto a dirt path. Follow this path through **As Carizas (8.7km)** to Dumbría.*

9.7 Dumbría A H 🍴🛒➕€
Pop. 3,000, 📖 Celtic: "fortified town"
1. **A** Xunta (🛏26, €10): 🔷⊙, next to municipal 🏊, ☎981744001, ⊙1pm all year, 📶 at pool
2. **H** Casa a Pichona (€75/80): 🍴📶, Castro 8, ☎609649252 📍, <u>before Dumbría in Castro</u>
3. **H** O Argentino (€35-45): 🍴🔷, ☎981744051, mixed reviews

17.1 A Grixa A H 🍴
A H O Cabanel (🛏14, €15/-/45): 🍴🔷 W D 📶 ⊙, A Grixa 39, ☎600644879 📍, ⊙all year
H Liñeiros (€90-125 🛏): 📶, A Grixa 29, ☎638281829 📍

9.7 Dumbría has a well-designed albergue, funded by the owner of the Zara clothing store chain. *Walk past the albergue into town past the 17th-century Iglesia de Santa Eulalia. Continue on the main road, which crosses under the highway where it becomes a dirt track up through **Trasufe (13.6km)**, with its Capela a Virxe do Espino. There is a spring with purported healing power behind the bus stop. Local people tie pieces of cloth to the tree as a prayer ritual. Continue east on a paved road over the bridge crossing the Río Castro and go R at the Y on minor road into **A Pelexa** 🍴🛒 **(16.1km)**. Turn L in town past mini market Agrodosio through the hamlet of **A Grixa (17.2km)**, with its roadside crucero and Igrexe de San Cibran. Turn L after Grixa, then R on a dirt path to Quintáns.*

OLVEIROA TO MUXÍA — 3A

21.3 Quintáns houses the modest Capilla de San Isideo. *Turn L and leave town on a dirt road. Pass by a massive hórreo with 22 stone supports! Pass **Ozón (21.7km)** to the Iglesia de San Martiño with a Romanesque apse and ruins of a Benedictine Monastery. After town, take a hard L turn through **Vilar de Sobremonte (23.0km)** on the road and turn R on a footpath. Come to a paved road close to the sea; turn L into **Os Muiños (27.0km)**.* Pass through this village, which has a panadería (bread shop) for provisions. *Leave town on the paved road, then straight on a grassy trail crossing the highway through Moraime.*

21.3 Quintáns H Pop. 240
H **Pensión Plaza** (€40/52): 🍴 📶,
Quintáns-Muxia, ☎981750452

21.7 Ozón A
A **Et Suseia** (💤10, €15-18): 🇰 W D O,
Lugar Pedragás 1, ☎689946840, ⏲Mar-Oct

25.1 Merexo H
H **Pensión Atlántico** (€40): 🍴🇰 📶, Merexo 108,
☎659133177

28.0 Moraime H
H **Monasterio de Moraime** (💤58, €100+):
🍴 W D 📶, ☎881076055, monastery from 1100s

28.0 Moraime was the site of the Iglesia de San Xiao de Moraime, an influential medieval monastery. *Turn R after town and cross the highway onto an small dirt road to pass the **Capela de San Roque (28.8km)** with a stone crucero in the forest. Continue on the dirt path through **Chorente (29.5km)**. The path will emerge on a boardwalk along the sea. Follow the shore into **Muxía (32.8km)**, and arrows out to the church on the northern edge of town (see p. 60-61).*

Huge hórreo after Quintáns

4

FINISTERRE TO MUXÍA

28.7km (17.8mi)
▲ 606m / ▼ 606m

⊙ **7-8 Hours**
Difficulty:
P 53%, 15.2km
U 47%, 13.5km

A Albergues:
As Lires 13.5km
Muxía 28.7km

Iglesia de Nosa Señora da Barca in Muxía

Roam the wild coastal moors and idyllic countryside on this less-traveled route. Marvel at the seaside church of Muxía and mysterious rock formations.

☀ This is a pleasant and isolated stage, the path winds through forest and village with the sea often in sight. Several cafés provide refreshment. To stay in the Xunta albergue in Muxía and receive a certificate of completion (*Muxiana*, p. 61), remember to **get a stamp in As Lires**. The path is less traveled than Finisterre and has a sense of wildness about it.

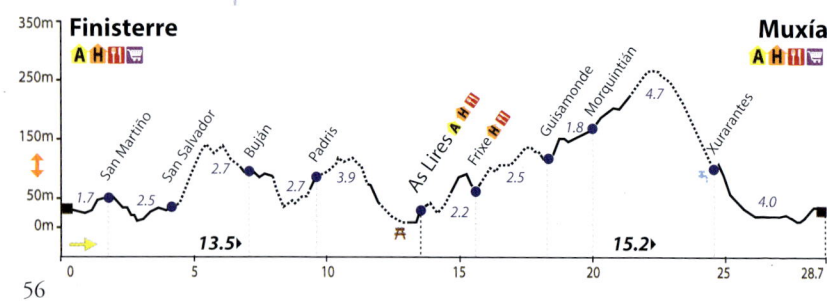

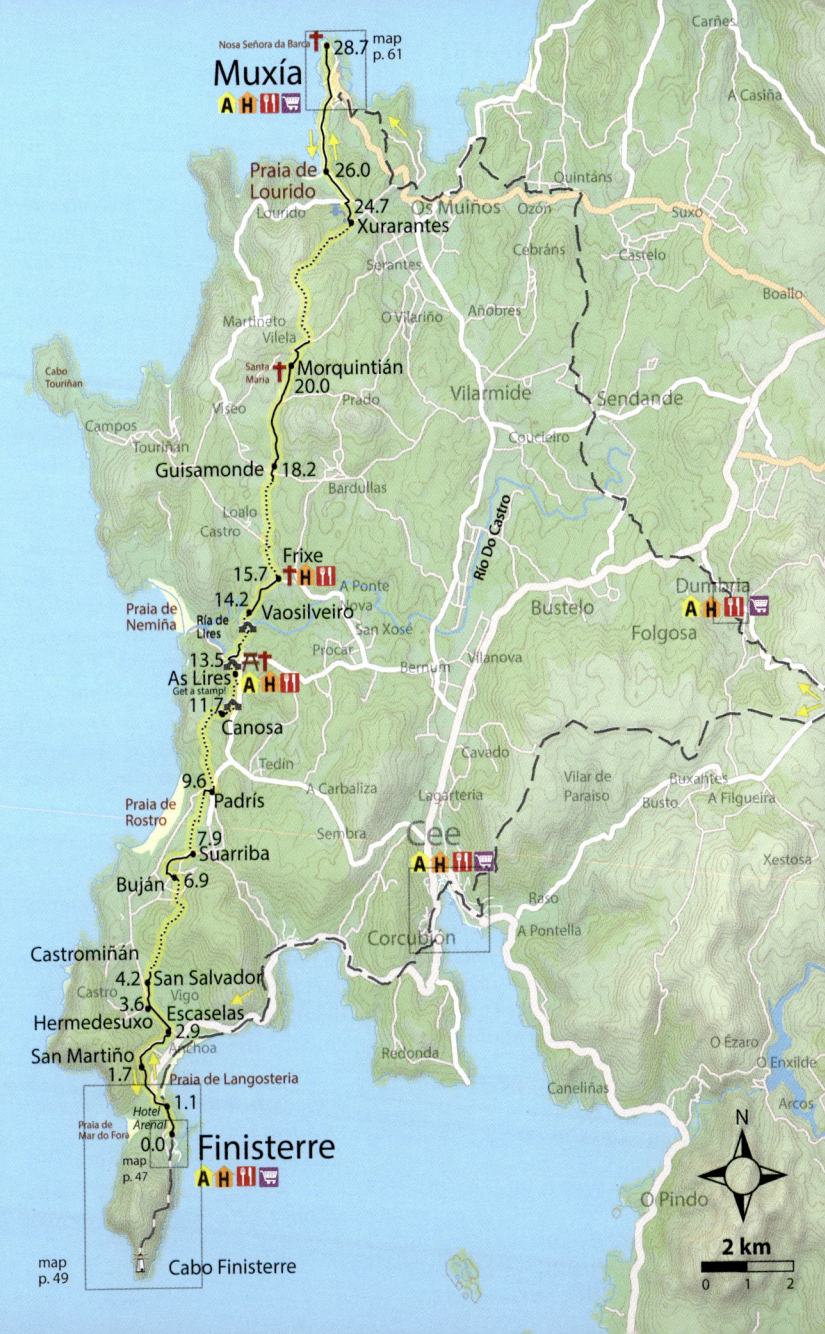

4 CAMINO FINISTERRE

Finisterre or Muxía? The choice is yours

0.0 *From the Finisterre Xunta albergue, walk up Rúa Catalina past the Concello and post office (maps p. 271 and p. 273). Continue along the main road and turn L on Aldea San Marín de Abajo at a bus shelter after the sign for Hotel Arenal (a Camino marker reads San Martiño, the next town, 1.1km). Stay straight through lower **San Martiño (1.7km)** past a housing development and then through upper San Martiño. Pass cornfields until going through **Escaselas (2.9km)**; turn L at a crossroads. Continue straight through **Hermedesuxo (3.6km)**, which has a stone crucero. At the crossroads, take the diagonal R into **San Salvador (4.2km)**, past Hotel Dugium. At the far end of town, the road turns to dirt and continues straight past an hórreo. Wind through a eucalyptus forest before passing through Rapadoiro and back onto an earthen track to **Buján (6.9km)**. After town, turn R on a paved road past a lumber factory into the forest. Continue on dirt through **Suarriba (7.9km)**, then turn L on a track with views of the sea. Meet the paved road to walk uphill, then turn L onto a dirt road with many yellow arrow markers at **Padrís (9.6km)**. The trail is paved through **Canosa (11.7km)**, then turns off to the L on dirt. Cross a small bridge to enter As Lires.*

13.5 As Lires is such a small town that the accommodations have no street addresses—ask around if you have trouble finding one. ⚠ **Make sure you get a stamp in As Liras**. The Xunta albergue in Muxía requires this stamp to prove you didn't arrive by bus. There is a stone crucero and church (Igrexa San Esteban). *Walk through Lires on the main road, then turn off onto a smaller road that will turn into a dirt path. Cross over a new bridge—look to the L to see the stepping stones that until recently pilgrims used to ford the river.*

13.5 As Lires 🅐 🅗 🍴 - get a stamp!
Pop. 165, 📖 Galician: "the lyres"
🅐 🅗 **As Eiras** (📞22, €18/65/70): 🅗 🅦 🅓 📶, ☎981748180, popular cafe
🅗 **Fragas de Canteira** (€55/70): 📶, Lires 94, ☎669033759 📝
🅗 **Liresca** (€57-92/62-98): 📶, Lires 31, ☎661464345 📝
🅗 **Casa Lourido** (€65): 📶, ☎981748348 📝
🅗 **Casa Luz** (€45/55): 📶, ☎981748924 📝
🅗 **Casa Jesus** (€58/69): 🍴 📶, ☎981748393 📝

FINISTERRE TO MUXÍA 4

*Enter tiny **Vaosilveiro (14.2km)** and continue on the dirt path that meets with a paved road. Turn L and then a quick R to cross the highway and pass through the outskirts of **Frixe, (15.7km)**, with Romanesque Iglesia de Santa Leocadia onto a dirt path. A sharp L downhill goes into **Guisamonde (18.2km)** on the paved road. Follow the paved road past a crucero and water fount (non-potable) into **Morquintián (20.0km)**, with its Romanesque Iglesia de Santa María. Continue on the paved road until it comes to a T. Turn R (ignoring the old cement maker), then turn off to the L on a dirt path. Continue through forest into **Xurarantes (24.7km)**. Turn L in town on a paved road curving around the forest. For the fastest way into Muxía, continue on the road. If you'd like to visit the attractive beach of **Praia de Lourido (26.0km)**, follow the markers straight on a dirt path that will turn to sand. There is not a clear path here so walk toward the water, and turn R to rejoin the main road.*

Enter Muxía via the sidewalk along the main road. To go directly to the Xunta albergue, turn R at the sign on Rúa Os Malatos and follow signs uphill through town to the albergue. To head to the church and seaside promenade, follow arrows on the west side of town out towards the northern point (map on p. 61).

> **15.7 Frixe**
> **Casa Ceferinos** (€70-90): Frixe 11, ☎981748965

O Camiño dos Faros (Lighthouse Camino) is a rugged and challenging 200-km route along the Costa da Morte between Finisterre and Malpica. The route features views of the spectacular rocky sea coast, numerous historic lighthouses, and picturesque fishing villages. GPS tracks are available for download, as the route waymarking can be challenging. Accommodations are in hotels and guesthouses.

More information at **caminodosfaros.com**

Muxía coast line on the western side

28.7 Muxía A H 🛒 ✚ ℹ️ 🅰️

Pop. 6,634, 📖 Archaic: "the monks"

1. **A** Xunta (🛏32, €10): 🍳, Enfesto, 📞610264325, 🕐1pm all year
2. **A** Da Costa (🛏8, €15/35/45): 🍳 W 📶, Doctor Toba 33, 📞676363820 📋, 🕐all year
3. **A H** Muxía Mare (🛏16, €16/-/45): 🍳 W D 📶, Castelao 14, 📞981742423 📋, 🕐all year
4. **A** @Muxía (🛏41, €15): 🍴 🍳 W D 📶, Enfesto 12, 📞609615533 📋, 🕐all year
5. **A H** Arribada (🛏38, €18/48/64): 🍳 W D 📶, José María del Río 30, 📞981742516 📋, 🕐all year
6. **A H** Bela Muxía (🛏52, €16/-/70): 🍳 W D 📶 ⊙, Encarnación 30, 📞687798222 📋, 🕐all year
7. **H** La Cruz (€85): 🍴 📶, López Abente 44, 📞981742084 📋, with sea views
8. **H** Hábitat Cm Muxia (€54/59): 📶, Real 40, 📞981742148 📋
9. **H** A de Loló (60-75): 🍴 📶, Virxe da Barca 37, 📞981742422 📋

28.7 Muxía is a picturesque fishing town located on a small peninsula, known for its fish and handmade lace. Muxía is especially known for its church, **Nosa Señora da Barca** ("Our Lady of the Boat"), a rustic church built over the rocky shore mere meters from the crashing waves. Legend has it that Mary appeared here in a stone ship to deliver a message to a discouraged Saint James. She informed him that he had been successful and should return to Jerusalem, his mission in Spain complete. She also gave him the image of herself displayed in the church. The second Sunday in September is 🎉 *La Festa de Nosa Señora da Barca*, one of the most important celebrations in Galicia. Thousands come from far and wide to visit the church, dance, sing, eat *caldareta* (fish stew), and parade the virgin through the streets. Sadly, the church building was severely damaged by fire after being struck by lightning on Christmas day in 2013 but has since been sensitively restored.

View of Muxía from Monte Corpiño

The large rocks outside the church are said to be the remains of her boat—*Pedra dos Cadris* represents her sail, the kidney-shaped *Pedra do Timón* the rudder, and *Pedra da Abalar* (a rocking stone similar to those in Finisterre) represents the hull. The rocking stone was used in pre-Christian times to determine the guilt of an accused party, and it continues rocking even after being broken during a storm in the 1970s. One legends says that when thieves were trying to rob the church, the stone rocked back and forth so loudly that the neighbors awoke and chased away the thieves. There is also the *Pedra dos Namorados* (Lovers' Rock) where couples come to declare their love.

Walk out to the sanctuary via a very pleasant promenade on the northeast side of the peninsula passing the 14th-century Marine-Gothic style **Iglesia de Santa María de Muxía**. Return by walking up the hill behind the church past the monument remembering the tragic Prestige oil spill of 2002. Walk up to the top of **Monte Copino** for an elevated view. This return path is known as the *Camiño da Pel* ("Way of the Skin") because pilgrims would wash themselves in a nearby fountain before entering the church.

Be sure to stop by the helpful **ⓘ Tourist Information** (☏981742365, ⊙variable hours). Present your credencial at the nearby library to receive the *Muxíana*, a decorative certificate of completion similar to the *Compostela*. The *Muxíana* is also available at the Xunta and Bela Muxía albergues.

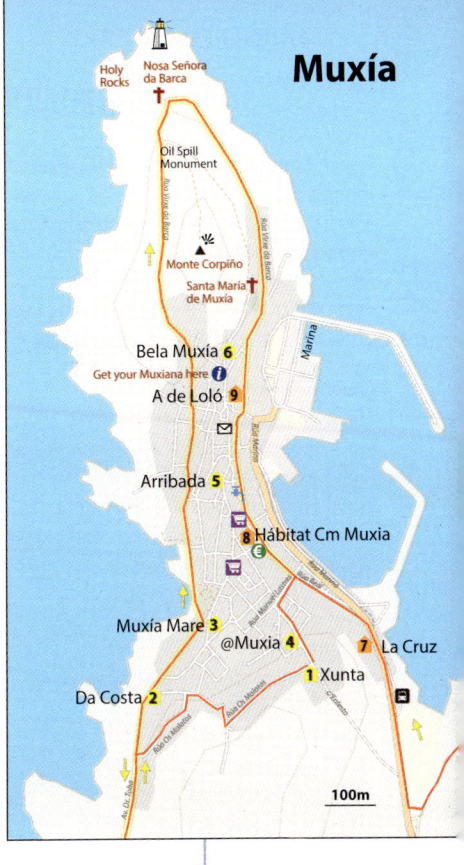

Transportation Muxía to Santiago:
There are several buses a day operated by **Monbus** (€6.70, 2-3 hours, ☏900929192).

For more options, take a bus to Cee, which has more buses per day to Santiago.

CAMINO FINISTERRE

Spanish Phrasebook

Local Languages: The main language you'll hear on the Camino is Spanish, though each region has at least one other official language, such as Galician in Galicia. Many local people along the Camino do not speak English. Learning some phrases in Spanish will greatly enhance your experience and reflects a respect for local culture that is often much appreciated. But don't let not speaking Spanish deter you from the Camino. Below is a very basic phrase list; <u>a more comprehensive phrasebook is available on our website.</u>

Greetings and Small Talk
Hello - *hola*
Goodbye/see you later - *adiós/hasta luego*
Good morning - *buenos días*
Good afternoon/evening - *buenas tardes*
Good night - *buenas noches*
Yes/no/maybe - *sí/no/quizás*
Please - *por favor*
How are you? - *¿Cómo estás?*
I am fine. - *Estoy bien.*
Where are you from? - *¿De dónde eres?*
I'm from... - *Soy de...*
 The USA - *Los Estados Unidos*
 Canada - *Canadá*
 England - *Inglaterra*
 Ireland - *Irlanda*
 Australia - *Australia*
 South Africa - *Sudáfrica*
Thank you - *gracias*
You're welcome - *de nada*
Excuse me - *disculpa*
Nice to meet you. - *Mucho gusto.*
I (don't) understand/Do you understand? - *(No) Entiendo/¿Entiendes?*
Do you speak English? - *¿Habla Inglés?*
I don't speak Spanish- *No hablo Español*
Please speak more slowly. - *Por favor, hable más despacio.*
One minute, please. - *Un momento, por favor.*
Walk well/happy trails - *Buen camino!*

What time does it open/close? - *¿A qué hora abre/cierra?*
Where is (are) the...? - *¿Donde está(n) …?*
 bathroom - *los servicios*
 hospital - *el hospital*
 a hostel – *un albergue*
Where can I find water? - *¿Dónde puedo encontrar agua?*
Do you have wifi? - *¿Tiene wifi? (wee-fee)*
Password - *contraseña, clave*

Problems - *problemas*
I'm lost. - *Estoy perdido.*
Help! - *Ayúdame!/Socorro!*
Call the police! - *Llama a la policía!*
Call a doctor! - *Llama a un médico!*
I need a doctor/dentist. - *Necesito un doctor/un dentista*
Go away! - *Véte!*
Leave me alone! - *Déjame en paz!*
Medicine - *medicamentos*
Pharmacy - *farmacia*
Medical center/clinic - *centro de salud*
Blister - *ampolla*
Fracture/sprain - *fractura*
I'm sick. - *Estoy enfermo/a...*
I'm allergic to - *Tengo alergia a...*
Penicillin - *la penicilina*
Bee sting - *picadura de abeja*
Beg bugs - *los chinches*
Pain - *dolor*

Notes

About the Authors

The authors with their children in Dolly Sods, West Virginia.

Anna Dintaman and **David Landis** are the cofounders of Village to Village Press and bring over 15 years of experience working with walking and cycling routes in Europe, the Middle East and Asia, as well as in their home area in the Shenandoah Valley of Virginia. Both are avid hikers and cyclists, with experiences ranging from backpacking Patagonia and Nepal, to hiking in the Middle East and biking across the USA. David cofounded the Jesus Trail, a hiking trail that connects sites from the life of Jesus and developed the TransVirginia gravel bikepacking route.

They have shared a deep love for the Camino since they each first took a 500-mile journey on the Camino Francés in 2009. They enjoy introducing their children to the joys of walking, the outdoors, and learning from other cultures.

Feedback welcome: info@villagetovillagepress.com

facebook.com/caminoguidebooks
instagram.com/caminoguidebook

Village to Village Press specializes in publishing guidebooks and supporting trail development projects worldwide.

CaminoGuidebook.com
Visit for free planning information including easy online booking, digital interactive maps, GPS tracks for navigation and frequently asked questions.

Kindle versions also available

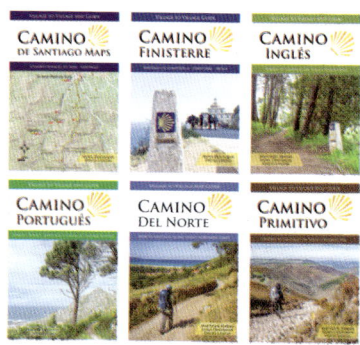